How to Grow Juicy
Tasty Tomatoes

Annette Welsford & Lucia Grimmer

Notes

How to Grow Juicy Tasty Tomatoes

Published by

Commonsense Marketing Pty Ltd
27 Anakie Drive,
Cornubia, Qld, 4130 Australia
info@bestjuicytomatoes.com

Copyright

Commonsense Marketing Pty Ltd, 2006

ISBN: 978-0-646-47067-2
Printed in China by Everbest

This book has been produced to provide basic information to home growers.

The information is general in nature and the authors are not responsible for the application of the principles in any particular case, as the contents or applications may need to be modified for the particular site and circumstances.

The information contained within this book has been carefully researched and is provided with care and in good faith. However the authors will not be held liable for any failure or damage to tomato crops or equipment which may result from the information provided.

Every effort has been made to obtain permission and provide a source reference for material used which is not the authors' own material.

Introducing the Authors

This book was written by two tomato growing enthusiasts in Brisbane, Australia.

Lucia Grimmer holds a Masters Degree in Plant Pathology and works as a technical nutrition specialist in the fertilizer industry. She has studied at many universities including those in the USA and has worked in a research capacity in both government and commercial organizations.

She is author of several scientific papers and technical disease and nutrition manuals. Lucia has won several awards from farming magazines for her technical articles.

Originally from Zimbabwe, Lucia and her husband owned a 1500 ha farm where they grew commercial and horticultural crops including tomatoes before they migrated to Australia. As a specialist in plant disease and nutrition, every day Lucia provides professional advice to commercial growers of tomatoes.

Annette Welsford has a partial degree in Horticulture and a Post Graduate Certificate in marketing. Having lived in the cold, temperate and hot parts of Australia and the UK, she has gained experience over the years with gardening in a variety of climates.

Annette also worked for a fertilizer company where she was responsible for developing, editing and publishing a range of technical manuals on nutrition and fungal diseases for a wide range of horticultural crops including tomatoes.

Her husband, originally from the southern tip of New Zealand is also an avid vegetable gardener. He's grown many tomato crops over the years throughout New Zealand and is now experiencing the delights of being able to grow tomatoes all year round in the sub-tropics.

Message from the Authors

This book evolved one hot summer afternoon over a glass or two of wine accompanied by a selection of delicious tomato based savouries.

We were reflecting on the extraordinary number of people who asked us for "inside secrets" or "magic tips" to growing tasty tomatoes successfully.

Friends often lamented that searching the internet provided masses of tomato hits, but the information provided was either too technical or too general. There didn't seem to be one site which catered for all the issues faced by tomato growers. To have all their questions answered they needed to conduct a lot of research and try and make sense out of conflicting advice.

So we undertook online market research ourselves and received enthusiastic feedback from tomato growers all over the world. A few months later

"How to Grow Tasty Juicy Tomatoes" was finally born!

The book is a one stop resource for anyone wanting to grow tomatoes at home.

The Quick Start Guide provides the basics of soil preparation, variety selection, nutrition, pest and disease control, watering and cultivation. It's designed to make it easy to get started. Here the novice tomato grower will find everything needed to get going with their first crop.

The enthusiast who's hungry for more information will not be disappointed either. The rest of the book provides the nitty gritty technical details needed to avoid the more common problems which most tomato growers face at some time or other.

Introduction

One of life's most sensual experiences is to go out to the tomato garden on a warm afternoon and pick a fresh, sun-ripened tomato.

The sun-kissed, rounded globe with its satiny skin fills your hand. The glowing colour delights the eye and the spicy aroma intoxicates your senses. Eaten then and there out of hand or sliced into a salad in the kitchen, a tomato offers a blend of colour, flavour and aroma that offers the single best reason to keep a home garden. It is that piquant aroma that truly differentiates a home grown fruit from store-bought.

Modern tomato breeders, growers and shippers try hard to bring a convincing approximation of fresh tomatoes to grocery shelves. Today's premium greenhouse-grown fruit is left under special lights to change colour on the vine and picked in multiple-fruit clusters with the green-leaved calyx intact. This is all done to convince buyers that they are truly vine-fresh. However they are at least several days from the vine, and have spent time sitting around in 70%-humidified, low-oxygen refrigeration.

The newest golfball-to-baseball-sized fruit are specially bred to redden through to the core and develop some sweetness and a soft internal texture.

But since genetic engineering has improved shelf life, these tomatoes have developed a tough skin and flesh to withstand shipping conditions that would turn an old-time vine-ripened garden variety to mush.

During the several days to three weeks spent in refrigerated shipping (and perhaps a week to another month of store display), they lose the spark of life and the ability to ripen seed or flesh any further, along with nearly all of their natural fragrance.

The typical supermarket "fresh" tomato has a vastly improved shelf life, appearance and eating quality. But it is still DOA - a corpse. It holds its gene-spliced shape, colour and superficial appearance of freshness, but gradually loses the flavour, nutrients and wonderful intoxicating aroma of the living thing. From the moment it's picked – senescence commences.

It's a sad fact of life that the most popular of all vegetables – the humble tomato – has been bred and modified so much that it doesn't taste or smell anything like it used to.

But all is not lost!

By purchasing this book you have taken the first important step in recovering your right to enjoy "real" tomatoes.

You will discover the wonderful initiatives that tomato lovers of the world have taken to keep the original tomato taste alive. We've sifted through reams and reams of research, data and anecdotes to ensure that home gardeners all over the world are equipped with the essential facts for growing the juiciest tastiest tomatoes possible.

v

Contents

1. History

In 2004 the top tomato producing countries of the world were China, USA, Turkey, India, Italy, Egypt, Spain, Iran, Brazil and Mexico, in that order.

The tomato has origins traced back to the early Aztecs around 700 A.D; therefore it is believed that the tomato is native to the Americas. What is now one of the world's favourite vegetables wasn't always so beloved. Called 'pomo d'oro', or "golden apple", in Italian, the tomato had a more sinister reputation in northern Europe and the United States where it was known as the stinking golden apple or wolf peach due to the long-held belief that it was poisonous.

One 17th-century cookbook said that although it was safe but "not advisable" to eat a cooked tomato, consuming a raw one would cause instantaneous death. The tomato's lethal reputation lasted until the early 1800s, even though Mediterranean countries had long before taken advantage of the tomato's culinary properties (they arrived in the 1500s and the first cookbook recipe with tomatoes was printed in 1692).

It didn't become widely grown in the US until the 1820s after Colonel Robert Johnson ate a basketful of tomatoes in public without ill effect.

At the turn of the 20th Century most families grew their own vegetables and fruit, but as people moved from the country to the city, more and more began to buy food rather than to grow it themselves. Specialist growers who were market-oriented sprang up close to the cities and chose higher-yielding varieties for commercial sale. The profit motive became the major criterion for plant improvement.

In the 1950s the emergence of supermarkets and refrigeration meant that warmer climate crops such as tomatoes, capsicums and melons became available in colder climates during out-of-season periods. New strains with tougher skins were bred to slow the ripening process and increase shelf life. Commercial hybrid seeds, costing 5-25 times as much as garden varieties, began to emerge to meet supermarket needs. National supermarket buyers encouraged the growth of "mega" farms to supply all states with identical produce, so hybrid commercial seeds took over from the regionally adapted garden heirlooms, which were consumer driven.

The advent of Genetically Modified Food is a revolutionary change to our food that offers no nutritional improvement, but increases the profitability and market power of global seed and chemical companies. Changes include incorporation of pesticides and weedicides within the DNA of the plant. If the ingredients and chemicals were properly labelled, like our processed food, some might be defined as pesticides!

In 1820 Robert Johnson of Salem, USA ate a tomato in front of a huge crowd to prove it wasn't poisonous.

1

2. Vegetable or Fruit?

An interesting aspect of tomato history is the classic debate: Is the Tomato a Fruit or Vegetable?

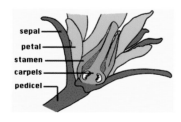

Figures 1 and 2.
Cross section of a tomato flower

Is a tomato a fruit or vegetable? I guess that depends on whom you are asking. In botany, a fruit is the ripened ovary—together with seeds—of a flowering plant. In many species, the fruit incorporates the ripened ovary and surrounding tissues. Fruits are the means by which flowering plants disseminate seeds.

By definition, a fruit is the edible plant structure of a mature ovary of a flowering plant. If eaten raw, some are sweet like apples, but the ones that are not sweet such as tomatoes, cucumbers, peppers, etc. are commonly called vegetables.

In 1893, because of a tariff dispute, the US Supreme Court settled the argument; although "botanically speaking tomatoes are the fruit of the vine," they were vegetables both "in the common language of the people" and in use since they were served with the main course or in soup.

The Latin name for the original wild tomato, *Lycopersicon esculentum* (of the family Solanaceae), means "edible wolf peach".

The tomato is classified in the division Magnoliophyta, class Magnoliopsida, order Solanales, family Solanaceae.

Tomato fruits exhibit all of the common characteristics of berries. The fruit develops from the ovary of the flower. The tomato is fleshy due to the pericarp walls and skin. Finally there are several seeds in each tomato (Weier et al., 1982).

Tomato plants have yellow flowers that, in full bloom, are generally less than an inch in diameter.

If we take a look at a longitudinal section through a tomato flower we can see that the tomato flower is organized in four whorls of organs (see Figures 1 and 2). The pedicel is the stem that supports the flower.

The male reproductive organs, the stamens, which house pollen production, sit inside the petals.

The tomato carpels are green. A carpel is where fertilization takes place. The ovules which will develop into seeds are protected in the carpel.

Fertilization takes place in the reproductive organs of the flower. The female organs, comprised of stigma, style, and ovary, collectively are called the pistil. The male organs consist of the anther and filament and are collectively called the stamen.

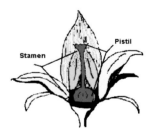

Figure 3: Reproductive organs

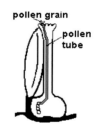

Figure 4: fertilisation

The tomato flowers of most commercial cultivars are self pollinating (Ho and Hewitt 1986). The pollen from the anther is transferred to the stigma of the same flower. Tomato flowers will be cross pollinated occasionally.

When this occurs the pollinator is usually the bumble bee (Hayward 1938).

Once the pollen grain has landed on the stigma the tube cell of the pollen grain elongates to form a tube. This tube reaches down the style all the way to one of the ovules in the ovary of the flower. Once the tube is formed the pollen grain's two sperm cells then travel down the tube into the embryo sac inside the ovule. (Campbell, 1993).

The ovule is fertilized through a process called double fertilization. It produces a diploid zygote and a triploid endosperm. The endosperm will store food for the embryo (Campbell, 1993). The fertilized ovule will become one of the seeds of the tomato fruit. The seed contains the embryo and the endosperm and is covered by a strong seed coat, called the testa. The testa is unique to tomatoes. The seed forms a thick outer epidermal layer. These cells partially break down; the "hairs" are what is left behind. These "hairs" collect a gelatinous material which gives the seeds a gooey membrane. This process forms the testa (Hayward 1938). The parts of the embryo are as follows: the shoot apex, two cotyledons (tomato is dicot), the hypocotyl and the root apex (Ho, Hewitt, 1986)

When the ovules in the ovary have been fertilized, the ovary begins to develop into the fruit. During the first stage of fruit development, cell division and enlargement results in slow growth. After 2~3 weeks of slow growth, rapid growth begins, during which time the cells continue to enlarge. Rapid growth continues for 3~5 weeks

culminating in the mature green stage. At this point the tomato has accumulated the majority of its final weight (Ho and Hewitt 1986).

Within two days of the beginning of the mature green stage the colour begins to change. The green pigment becomes lighter and a faint yellow-orange colour appears (Ho and Hewitt 1986).

As the fruit begins to have more of an orange pigment on the outside, many metabolic changes are occurring on the inside. The pulp of the fruit softens as a result of enzymatic digestion of the cell walls. The placental tissue, which fills much of the locular spaces and the areas around the ovules, becomes degraded and assumes a gelatinous consistency (Grierson and Kader 1986).

Once the tomato has reached maturity an abscission layer forms between the calyx and the fruit, ultimately resulting in the fruit falling off the pedicel.

Source:

Most of the text and all of the photos and diagrams in this section were provided with the kind permission of:
Thomas L. Rost, Professor Emeritus
Section of Plant Biology
College of Biological Sciences
University of California
Davis, CA 95616
tlrost@ucdavis.edu
http://www-plb.ucdavis.edu/labs/rost/Tomato/tomhome.html

3. Health Effects

Just eating one tomato a day provides one-third of your daily requirement of vitamin C and one to two grams of fibre.

Oil based cooked tomato products - like tomato paste and tomato sauce aid the release of lycopene

Tomatoes are a good source of vitamin C and potassium. They also pack plenty of the phytochemicals that provide disease prevention benefits. Tomatoes are high in lycopene (a powerful antioxidant) and phenolic compounds. In our diet, 95% of lycopene intake comes from tomatoes and tomato products. It is also found in watermelon, pink grapefruit, papaya and rosehip.

Lycopene is the carotenoid that makes tomatoes red. It appears that lycopene can reduce the risk of certain cancers, the eye disorder age-related macular degeneration, atherosclerosis and sun damage to the skin.

Men who eat two or more servings of tomato products average a 35 percent reduction in prostate cancer risk.

Lycopene helps women guard against cervical intra-epithelial neoplasia, (CIN), tumorous tissue growth in the cervix according to research from the University of Illinois at Chicago. Lycopene is a powerful inhibitor of the growth of breast, endometrium (inner lining of the uterus) and lung cancer cells.

Lycopene is better absorbed by the body when it is cooked with some oil. The cooking helps to break down the cell walls of the tomato releasing the lycopene and the oil helps increase its absorption. Japanese scientists found that mixing tomato juice into the drinking water of mice completely prevented them suffering emphysema triggered by tobacco smoke.

Tomatoes also contain Lutein. Lutein is found in the retina of our eyes so it needed for healthy vision. Lutein also appears to lower the risk of cataracts and macular degeneration. Lutein may also help to prevent or slow down the thickening of arteries that is called atheroscler osis. Atherosclerosis is a major risk for cardiovascular disease.

Tomato products are beneficial in aggressive cancers that have also spread to other parts of the body.

Further reading:

Giovannucci, Edward et al., *"Intake of Carotenoids and Retinol in Relation to Risk of Prostate Cancer,"* Journal of the National Cancer Institute, Advanced Research Press, Inc. 1999. Hauppauge, N.Y.

Tomato Research Council, Article, *"Lycopene in the American Diet,"* Undated

Hanley, Daniel Q., *"Tomatoes, Oranges, Pasta and Soybeans Studied as Cancer fighters,"* AP, April 14, 1997

Kumpulainen, Jorma T. et al, *"Natural Antioxidants and Food Quality in Atherosclerosis and Cancer Prevention,"* Royal Society of Chemistry Information Services and Scheer, James F., *"Tomato Power! Lycopene: The Miracle Nutrient That Can Prevent Aging, Heart Disease and Cancer,"* Advanced Research Press, Inc. 1999. Hauppauge, N.Y.

Meres-Perlman, Julie A., Ph.D., *"Serum Antioxidants and Age-Related Macular Degeneration in a Population-Based Case-Control Study,"* Archives Ophthalmology, December, 1995, Vol. 113:1518-1523.

Aviram, Michael, Ph.D., *"Lycopene and Antherosclerosis,"* A publication of Technion-Israel Institute of Technology and Scheer, James F., *"Tomato Power! Lycopene: The Miracle Nutrient That Can Prevent Aging, Heart Disease and Cancer,"* Advanced Research Press, Inc. 1999. Hauppauge, N.Y.

http://www.tomatofest.com/tomato_health_facts.html

http://www.wptc.to/tomato-health-wptc.aspx

4. Quickstart

Getting started is easy. The fastest way is to buy some tomato seeds or seedlings, plant them after the last frost and watch them grow!

What to grow

Choosing the variety is important. You need to decide what characteristics are the most important to you, as well as the climate and disease susceptibility in your area. No one variety will perform best across all planting seasons and regions. Issues such as fruit firmness, size, shape, flavour and plant growing habits need to be considered.

You also need to decide whether you want a 'jointed' tomato variety or not. In other words, do you want a tomato variety that retains its stalk when picked or one that comes away cleanly from its stalk when picked. Many commercial organic and gourmet tomato growers choose 'jointed' tomato varieties because the tomato with its stalk attached looks attractive to the buyer. However, most home gardeners and non-organic commercial growers choose 'jointless' varieties.

The next choice is whether you want a 'determinate' or 'indeterminate' variety. A determinate variety grows to a bush about 1 metre (3 feet) high. At this stage it stops growing and sets a concentrated crop of tomatoes which can be picked over a few weeks.

Indeterminate varieties keep growing and can reach a height of up to 5 metres (15 or more feet) when fully mature. The fruit from these can be picked over a period of 12 to 20 weeks. These varieties are frequently used by greenhouse producers. Many cherry tomato varieties are indeterminate.

There are also 'semi-determinate' varieties which grow to about 1.5 – 2 metres

(4 – 6 ft.) and set fruit over a longer period than determinate varieties. These are the best suited to home gardens. They generally require staking and the tomatoes are harvested over 2 – 6 weeks.

Seeds or seedlings?

Unless you are experienced at growing seeds, it is best to buy seedlings from a nursery. Seedlings are generally uniform in size and usually suffer very little from transplant shock when properly planted out.

Growing your own seeds to transplants requires experience, time and a certain amount of infrastructure. Generally you will need planting racks, soil or potting mix which contains the right mix of nutrients, sterilizing equipment, a mixer, seedling trays, potting area and (in colder climes) a plastic igloo.

How many seedlings?

The following spacing guide will enable you to roughly calculate how many seedlings you will need to fill your tomato plot.

Spacing: tomato plants should be planted about 50-90 cm (18 inches to 3 feet) apart in a row.

Should you decide to plant more than one row of tomatoes, the space between the rows should be about 1.5 – 2m (4 – 6ft). Gourmet and staked tomatoes are normally planted about 50 – 60cm (2ft) apart.

The more space you can give your plants, the better chance you will have for growing disease free tomatoes. Fungal diseases in particular thrive in moist conditions so try and maximise airflow around each bush.

When to grow

Tomatoes are quite sensitive to temperature. They are particularly susceptible to frost at all growth stages, even when they're fruiting. The fruit can crack during cold snaps, so you will need to keep an eye on the weather.

The best temperature for seed germination is usually between 20 and 30ºC, (68 and 86ºF) but decreases quickly at below 15ºC (60ºF) and above 30ºC (86ºF).

Tomato varieties differ in their sensitivity to temperature, which can affect their pollination and fruit set (growth of the tomato fruit).

The right temperature is important for germinating healthy seedlings.

The ideal temperature for fruit set is between 17 and 25ºC (62 and 77ºF). In borderline conditions, fruit may set without adequate pollination, however this can result in puffy and flat-sided fruit that contain few seeds.

For best pollination and fruit set, minimum night temperatures should be below 27ºC (80ºF) and daily maximums above 18ºC (64ºF). If the temperature exceeds 28ºC (82ºF) fruit can be softer and yellow or orange in colour, especially if there is not a lot of leaf cover.

Where to grow

Some gardeners may have no choice of site, but those that do need to consider a few issues.

Wind

Tomatoes are relatively tolerant of windy conditions, but the wind will cause staked tomatoes to chafe on the stake and will also increase water loss, unless mulch is used. The most critical stage is from fruit set onwards as tomatoes can be damaged from scuffing between fruit and stems. This causes light brown scabs on the fruit.

Windbreaks will help reduce these problems, but care needs to be taken that these wind breaks do not shade the crop and are far enough away that they do not interfere with the growth of the tomatoes.

Soil Erosion

Whilst a flat site is the best for growing tomatoes, some gardeners may be restricted to a sloping site. On steeply sloping sites water runoff carries away the good topsoil, causing erosion.

To reduce erosion:

1. Mulch the site, however take care not to mulch right against the tomato stems as this can cause stem rot

2. Grow a band of grass below the area of tomatoes

3. Run beds across the slope to minimize loss of soil and increase water infiltration

4. Dig a contour slope below the tomatoes to catch runoff water and soil

Crop rotation

Tomatoes belong to the same family as potatoes, egg fruit and capsicums. Hence they are subject to the same pests and diseases.

Crop rotation will help with avoiding disease build-up. Try not to grow tomatoes on the same patch where tomatoes and related crops have grown during the last three years.

Diseases can also move in the garden by hitching a ride on your spade as you turn over the soil or even on the bottom of your shoes. For those reasons, rotating in a small garden may be impractical. That's not to say there is nothing a gardener can do. Adding lots of organic matter to the soil such as compost or rotted manure will help break some pest cycles and give you some of the benefits of rotating.

If you have time in Autumn (Fall) plant a cover crop such as rye grass or oats. These cover crops will help control diseases. There is even evidence that indicates that some cover crops can actually work as a natural fumigant and kill some plant pathogens.

How to grow

Start your tomatoes off by sowing seeds in a pot or seed tray towards the end of Autumn (Fall). Leave them to germinate on a windowsill or somewhere that is warm and frost-free. If you prefer to buy seedlings, start at step 4.

1 How to sow

Fill a 7.5cm (3in) pot with seed mix, lightly firm the surface and water gently. Thinly scatter the seeds, cover with a small amount of compost and clearly label the pot. Keep the compost moist but not waterlogged - preferably using a light mist sprayer.

2 Handling seeds

Once they are large enough to handle, carefully prick out a single seedling using a dibber or a pencil, bringing as many roots as possible with it. Lift the seedling gently by holding a leaf. Avoid holding the stem as this is easily damaged.

3 Pricking out

Take the seedling and plant it in its own 7.5cm (3in) pot of seedling mix, gently pushing it into place. Water it gently and place in a warm, frost-free, well-lit location, remembering to turn the pot daily if it's on a windowsill.

4 Planting out

When risk of frost has passed, drive a stake around 2cm (0.75in) in diameter into a prepared garden bed. The soil should have been turned over with organic matter several weeks before transplanting.. Dig a hole a little deeper than the height of the plant's pot next to the stake, gently place the plant in the hole and firm in. Tomato cages, or trellises can be used for support in lieu of stakes. The tomato seedlings should be planted 45cm (18in) apart to allow the sun to reach the ripening fruits.

5 Staking

Use soft twine or special tomato ties to tie the plant's stem loosely to the stake. As the plant grows, check the ties regularly and loosen them occasionally to prevent stem damage. .

6 Remove sideshoots

Regularly nip out sideshoots that develop between the leaf and the stem using your thumb and finger. This helps to help channel the plant's energy into its fruits. Watering and regular feeding with a potassium based fertilizer will ensure a plentiful, healthy crop.

7 Harvesting

When the fruits have ripened, pick them by bending back the fruit at the notch on the stem. They can be eaten straight from the plant, or can be stored for up to a week in the fridge. Continue to water and feed the plant to help the remaining fruits mature.

Staking/pruning

Staking or trellising is a cultural technique carried in out in areas where humid or moist growing conditions would cause a high amount of disease or blemishes on the fruit. By training the plant up a stake or over a trellis, air circulation is encouraged and fruit are lifted away from the soil where fruit rotting occurs. Staking also allows pruning of plants which helps to increase fruit size.

In dry growing conditions, staking or trellising is not critical and a plastic mulch will often suffice. Staked crops are usually harvested more frequently over a longer growing period.

Watering

- Water thoroughly to encourage the tomato roots to seek water and nutrients deep in the soil. With an extensive, deep root system, the plants will hold up better during dry spells. When watering, soak the soil to a depth of at least 15-20 cm (6-8 inches).

- Water only when your plants need it. Tomatoes like moisture, but over watering is harmful. You not only waste water, but soggy soil will prevent the roots from getting the air they need. If your plants look a little wilted on a hot, summer afternoon, that's usually normal. They'll perk up overnight. If plants are wilted in the morning, don't wait -- water them! (However remember that certain diseases can also cause wilting.)

- A thorough soaking every four to five days on light, sandy soils and every seven to ten days on heavy soils is a good general guide for irrigating if you don't get enough rain.

- Water early in the day to cut down on evaporation losses and also to give your plants plenty of time to dry out. Wet foliage overnight may help trigger some diseases.

- With furrow irrigation, drip irrigation or soaker hoses, which all deliver water right at the soil surface and not on the leaves, you can water almost any time. Try to avoid watering at midday though, because that's when evaporation losses are highest.

- Trickle irrigation is the most easily controlled method of irrigation. The equipment is expensive, but is long lasting and saves growers time. It can also be scheduled to deliver constant amounts of water, which can help reduce the incidence of fruit cracking.

- Use mulch to reduce evaporation, improve water spread and uptake by the plants and reduce disease caused by rain and water splash.

Nutrition

All plants enjoy substantial amounts of organic matter – manure or compost in the soil. Organic matter holds nutrients in the soil so that they are not lost through leaching. It increases the amount of water your soil can hold as well as microbial activity in the soil, encouraging earthworms and creating a wonderful healthy soil system that produces nice sweet tomatoes.

To ensure that your tomato plants grow and fruit properly,

Understanding Fertilizers

All fertilizers are generally described by their analysis. This usually consists of three figures that respectively label the % of Nitrogen (N), Phosphorus (P) and Potassium (K) in a product. The sequence of N, P and K never changes.

In the USA these units are designated as N - P_2O_5 – K_2O whilst in other countries (such as Australia) the units are N-P-K.

P_2O_5 means phosphate in the oxide form, as opposed to phosphorus (used in Australia) and K_2O is the oxide form of potassium whilst in Australia only K or potassium is used.

it is recommended that fertilizer is applied at three stages.

1. **Pre-planting:** Add organic matter and compost at least two - three weeks before planting out your seedlings. You can supplement the organic matter with a granular fertilizer which contains nitrogen, phosphorus and potassium. (See inset on page 16 for explanation of N-P-K and $N\text{-}P_2O_5\text{-}K_2O$). You can buy fertilizer which is already pre-mixed in various ratios (we suggest 5-10-10, 5-20-20 or 8-16-16) and work this into the soil about two weeks before planting.

2. **First Flower:** At this stage your plants may need a little bit of nitrogen and a larger portion of potassium to ensure they continue to flower and set lots of fruit. Try sprinkling the following amounts around your plants, taking care not to get any on the stems or lower leaves.

    Nitrogen (N) – 8g or 1.5 teaspoons/m^2 (0.2oz/ft^2)

    Potassium (K) – 20g or 4 teaspoons/m^2
    or in the USA **(K_2O)** 25g or 5 teaspoons/m^2 (.6oz/ft^2)

3. **Three weeks later:** repeat the application described above for first flower.

Note: liquid fertilizers (instead of granular) are also very effective, however care should be taken to dilute them in accordance with the instructions on the label, otherwise severe burning and death could occur.

Whenever you add fertilizer, it always advisable to thoroughly water it in. Your plants take up the nutrients when they are suspended in water, not when they are lying around the soil in granular form.

Giving your plants too little or too much fertilizer can reduce yields and cause other problems. Refer to the information on Nutrition Problems in Section 9.

Pests/diseases

Unfortunately tomatoes are susceptible to numerous pests and diseases, so it is wise to frequently inspect them.

If a plant does not look completely healthy, consult information on pests and diseases in Section 10 to identify the problem and take corrective action.

How to revive damaged plants

If cutworms, mice, slugs, the neighbour's dog or other hazards hack into your transplants, don't despair. If you get to the plant before the sun has baked the life out of it, cut an inch or so off the bottom of the stem and place the rest in a container of water out of direct sun for a week or so. It will sprout roots along the stem. Then transplant it back into garden and watch it grow.

Healthy nutritious soil helps make juicy tasty tomatoes

Tips for success

- Choose varieties which are suitable for your climate.

- Sow seeds six to eight weeks before the last frosts are expected.

- Clearly label the seed pots with the variety name and the date of sowing.

- Tomato seeds germinate best at 15°C to 20°C (59°F to 68°F). For home gardeners - a windowsill is ideal.

- Before planting out, harden off the plants by placing them outside during the day for at least a week. Dipping your seedling plug into a solution of seaweed will boost root growth.

- Water your plants regularly to prevent the fruits' skin from splitting.

- Stake your plants to reduce disease and damage from strong winds

- When 6 or 7 trusses have set fruit, remove the growing tip to hasten ripening.

- Regularly feed your plants to encourage growth and keep them healthy. Remember though they need different combinations of fertilizer at each growth stage.

- Remove weed competition from around the tomato plants during the summer.

- Keep an eye out for pests and take action before it is too late.

- Pick the fruits when they are fully ripe, to capture all the flavour.

- Rotate crops every year to reduce disease.

What is Thigmatropy?

Thigmatropy is the name for an effect where plants alter their growth habits as a result of being touched. It was first noticed in greenhouses where plants next to the aisles were found to grow sturdier and healthier. The cause was workers walking down the aisle brushing against the plants. You can stimulate thigmatropy by rubbing your hands or a stick across the tops of the plants a couple of times a day or by placing a fan so it blows gently across the seedlings.

Tomatoes and many other plants seem to respond to vibration in the air by growing more vigorously. This is similar to thigmatropy but the effect is caused by sound vibrations in the air.

5. Varieties

With over 10,000 known tomato varieties, choosing the right tomatoes for your climate and garden size will be an interesting task.

Heirloom varieties

Courtesy of Pastilla LaMannequine

This chapter introduces you to the different types of tomatoes and provides useful information on some of the more popular varieties.

There are many excellent tomato varieties available, ranging from new hybrids to tasty heirloom varieties. When selecting varieties you should consider productivity, freedom from fruit splitting and disease resistance.

The tomato varieties you pick should be a good fit for your climate because big, healthy plants produce better-tasting tomatoes.

Heirloom varieties are famous for their flavours, and equally notorious for growing well in some areas, but not in others.

With any tomato, foliage leads to lots of flavour, but be careful not to over-fertilise as this will produce lots of foliage and little fruit. Lush foliage is due to both nature (variety) and nurture (how the plants are grown).

Tomato varieties mature over a wide range of time spans, commonly from 75 days for early cherry types to 85 days for early full size fruit types, 100 days for medium, and 110 days for later, full season varieties from direct seeded plantings. Transplanted plantings would be about 25 days less. Research indicates that a temperature of 20-25°C (68-78°F) is ideal for optimal growth.

Tomatoes are described according to size, shape and the use of the fruit, the stage of the season that the fruit appears; and the growth habit of the plant.

Cherry tomatoes are the size of cherries or smaller.

Beefsteak varieties have large symmetrical fruit.

Oxhearts are pointed at the base and lobed at the top, similar to a heart.

Paste tomatoes have physical characteristics that make them suitable for sauces and chutneys.

Drying varieties tend to be cherry types, which have a minimum of moisture that dries rapidly. Stuffing varieties contain hollow cavities making them ideal for stuffing with your favourite filling.

Tomato varieties are classified as early, mid or late season, which refers to how long it is before the fruit appears after transplanting.

Early will be 55 – 70 days, mid will be around 75 - 90 days and late-season tomatoes produce fruit from around 100 – 120 days.

In regions with mild summers, selecting late-season varieties may limit the quantity of fruit produced before the end of the season. Once fruiting commences, many will continue to produce until frosts kill the plant.

More about Heirlooms

Originally, the term "heirloom" (in reference to gardening) was coined during the early 1970s to identify those vegetable and flower varieties that had originated with a particular family of people and had subsequently been passed down from one generation to the next up to modern day.

Typically these varieties were obtained from a single source who had maintained them for many years. Often these varieties were completely unique and had been limited to only one or two gardens per era. This not only made these varieties rare, but also made them very desirable by gardeners who revelled in the idea of preserving a small part of agricultural history and being one of only a few people with the variety (www.roguelands.com).

Tomato plants are naturally self pollinating and a general characteristic of self-pollinating plants is that they become genetically homozygous after many generations. Since they do not naturally outcross very often, seeds of a tomato will produce plants resembling the parents.

Early cultivars did not change much because of this property, and were kept in a family or community for long periods of time. Heirloom cultivars dating back over a hundred years are still grown today.

Most heirloom varieties are unique in size, shape or colour. Some are black, dark purple, or red with black shoulders, many are green, some have green stripes or are rainbow coloured, or shaped like peppers.

Of course there are orange and yellow cultivars too and everything in between. Some are cherry size, some are over 1 kilo (2 pounds).

Because heirloom tomatoes haven't been 'worked on' by plant breeders, they don't usually have much disease resistance. However many diseases can be essentially prevented or delayed by mulching the soil surface to prevent disease spores in the soil splashing up and infecting the young plants.

Mulching plus fungicidal sprays mean that heirlooms can usually be grown successfully in all but the very hot humid areas notorious for tomato disease.

Since 'heirloom' varieties have become popular in the past few years there have been liberties taken with the use of this term for commercial purposes. Heirloom tomato experts, Craig LeHoullier and Carolyn Male, Ph.D. have classified heirlooms into four categories:

- **Commercial Heirlooms:** Open-pollinated varieties introduced before 1940.

- **Family Heirlooms:** Seeds that have been passed down for several generations through a family.

- **Created Heirlooms:** Crossing two known parents (either two heirlooms or an heirloom and a hybrid) and dehybridizing the resulting seeds for however many years/generations it takes to eliminate the undesirable characteristics and stabilize the desired characteristics, perhaps as many as 8 years or more.

- **Mystery Heirlooms:** Varieties that are a product of natural

The famous Mortgage Lifter heirloom variety

Many heirloom cultivars have colourful histories. Consider the story regarding the cultivar Mortgage Lifter.

A West Virginian named Charlie owned a radiator repair shop that fell on hard times in the Great Depression as people abandoned their cars.

He used the four largest-fruited tomato plants he had and crossed them repeatedly among each other to create a plant that produced two pound fruits.

He sold plants for a dollar each, claiming one plant would feed a family of six. Within four years, he had made enough money to pay off the four thousand dollar mortgage on his house!

cross-pollination of other heirloom varieties.

(Note: All heirloom varieties are open-pollinated but not all open-pollinated varieties are heirloom varieties.)

More about Hybrids

A hybrid variety is produced when one type of tomato is crossed with another to produce a new variety with a mix of characteristics from its parents. Hybrid cultivars have come to dominate every area of tomato production, from large scale to backyard.

One drawback, as far as the home gardener is concerned, is that hybrid seed or plants must be purchased every year. Seed from hybrid plants, if propagated, will produce the F2 segregating generation causing plants to be very diverse and not at all like that parent. This is the very property that makes hybrids so attractive to seed producers since it ensures that customers must buy new seed each year.

Hybridisation may not directly reduce diversity, but indirectly its use by seed companies has caused this reduction. All of the old varieties of tomato are a common heritage of humanity, so that nobody owns them or has rights over them. The loss of varieties is of great concern because part of society's heritage is lost. There is less choice with fewer types offered, and varieties with distinctive and unique characteristics are lost.

The home gardener can however help turn the tide in the loss of varieties and preserve genetic diversity. One way is to purchase seed or plants from companies that offer heirloom

varieties and grow them at home. It can be great fun growing some of these obscure varieties with many surprises in store in terms of appearance and flavour. The other way home gardeners can help preserve then is to collect and save seed.

In meeting the particular needs of supermarket vegetables, hybrids became so altered as to be almost useless for gardeners, because gardeners want above all, tasty crops as well as early crops and late crops and continuity in between. Industrial agriculture wants crops that can be harvested all at once and shipped without loss over long distances.

Trials in Australia produced the following results[1]:

- Two varieties of heirloom tomato, Tigerella and Green Bell Pepper, produced twice the yield of the most popular and latest hybrid, Apollo.

- Popular American hybrid Celebrity was inferior in yield to Tigerella, fruiting 12 days later and also having the profound disadvantage of producing 68% of its fruit in one month, compared with Tigerella, causing an unnecessary glut.

Cold Climate Varieties[2]

The tomato is a sub-tropical plant and contrary to what some seed companies advertise, there is no such thing as a frost-resistant or frost-proof tomato variety.

As well as not being frost-proof, tomatoes cannot be grown

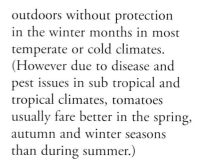

outdoors without protection in the winter months in most temperate or cold climates. (However due to disease and pest issues in sub tropical and tropical climates, tomatoes usually fare better in the spring, autumn and winter seasons than during summer.)

Tomatoes require sunlight and a good amount of heat to produce fruit, which ultimately means that equipment and facilities may be required in non tropical areas to grow tomatoes during the winter.

So with that in mind, what are "cold climate" tomatoes and what use are they? Simply put, a cold climate tomato is a variety which is ideally suited for climates which have a short growing season. Though many cold climate varieties can withstand cooler weather than others, their real value is in the fact that they mature much earlier than other varieties of tomatoes and are therefore suited for areas with shorter growing seasons and less than ideal climates.

That is not to say that growing tomatoes in the winter cannot be done, but it does require much planning and at least some equipment (lighting, heaters, a greenhouse, etc) to get good results. Alternatively, it can also be done indoors in a bare corner of the house, but this sometimes delivers less than satisfactory results without extra lighting.

In cold-climate areas, plant in spring after frost danger is past.

---

1 Trials conducted by Diggers Mail Order Seeds, Dromana, Victoria, Australia www.diggers.com.au

2. Cold climate variety information kindly provided by www.roguelands.com.

Ailsa Craig

seeds.thompson-morgan.com

Medium sized green back fruit of perfect size and shape early in the season with excellent deep colour and noted for its vigour.

Gem State

seedstrust.com

A cross between subarctic and a larger, beefsteak tomato. Compact, bush-type growth. Excellent for containers and patio gardens. Produces small 60gm (2 oz) fruits.

Harbinger

organiccatalog.com

One of the oldest and best flavoured tomatoes with a smooth thin skin. Ideal for ripening off the plant. Reliable producer which flourishes in most any garden.

Legend

seeds.thompson-morgan.com

Will produce a heavy crop of large glossy red fruits of up to 180g (6oz). The fruits are a slightly flatter shape, almost seedless, early ripening, and have excellent flavour.

Marmande

gardenandleisure.com

Popular old French variety developed by the Vilmorin Seed Co. Scarlet, lightly ribbed fruit, have the full rich flavour that is so enjoyed in Europe. Medium-large size fruit are produced even in cool weather.

Nepal

victoryseeds.com

Large, cold-tolerant beefsteak with intense, rich flavour. Original strain from Himalayan Mountains in Nepal. Bright-red, smooth, 280-340gm (10-12 oz.) fruits.

Orange King

victoryseeds.com

A large, early bright-orange slicer weighing up to 350 gm (3/4 pound). Tastes mild but tart and not sweet like you might expect. A determinate plant that sets well in high or low temperature conditions.

Paul Robeson

roguelands.com

This variety originated with a vegetable seed firm in Central Siberia. A gorgeous, dark and dusky-hued fruit with intensely sweet earthy taste; a luscious velvety smooth texture, beautiful skin, rich with juice. This marvellous plant will give you its perfect 7-10cm (3"- 4") fruit in only 65 days from planting.

Scotia

highmowingseeds.com

Developed in Nova Scotia, this high-quality red slicer will set fruit well even in cooler weather where most tomato varieties cannot. Smooth and firm with very good flavour, highly reliable.

Siberian

roguelands.com

A very early ripening tomato variety which performs exceptionally well every year in a short growing season. The plant is semi-determinate and produces a very large number of round, brilliant red, juicy fruits with excellent flavour for early variety.

Stupice

heirloomtomatopants.com

Indeterminate potato-leaf vines to 1.2m (4 feet). Smallish 85-170gm (3-6 oz) fruits. Very juicy fruits of excellent flavour. Good yield, very early, ideal in cool weather. Bears till frost.

Sub Arctic

seeds.thompson-morgan.com

One of the very earliest tomatoes, the compact plants produce lots of 55gm(2 oz) red fruit. It one of the best for cool conditions and will set fruit in lower temperatures than most. Ideal for hanging baskets.

Note: photos kindly provided with the permission of the companies listed alongside each variety. Seeds for these varieties are available from the company listed and in some cases also from other online seed companies - see p88.

Hot Climate Varieties

In hot climates, plant when temperatures begin to cool in early autumn. Although the tomato is a warm-hot climate plant, in very hot areas the heat can cause reduction in pollen germination, flower drop and failure to set fruit. Heat also leads to poorer quality fruit. New crop varieties have been developed that are heat tolerant. These varieties perform better in the heat because they possess more heat shock proteins (hsp).

Cosmonaut Volkov
highmowingseeds.com

A smooth and attractive, medium-large red tomato that has a full, rich flavour. The productive vines yield well even in hot weather, perfect for canning or slicing. This variety is from Dniepropetrousk, Ukraine, and was named after the first Russian Cosmonaut.

Floradade
victoryseeds.com

The Floradade was developed by the University of Florida to be resistant to the particular problems that affect tomatoes in humid areas. Nice-sized fruit are round and smooth; determinate plants are quite productive.

Homestead 24
victoryseeds.com

These determinate plants are large with heavy foliage and produce 200 gm (7-8 oz) meaty, firm, red fruits which are consistently uniform.

Marion F
rachelssupply.com

A vigorous vine resistant to leaf mould and gray leaf spot, the Marion produces smooth deep red 180gm (6oz) fruits.

Pink Accordian
readytogrow.co.uk

Large, pink, ruffled tomatoes sweet mild flavour that look extraordinary sliced. With a slightly hollow interior, they're also excellent for stuffing.

Ponderosa Pink
reimerseeds.com

Plant produces high yields of flavourful extra large 500gm (1 lb) pink beefsteak tomatoes. Tomatoes are almost seedless, low acidity and very meaty with a sweet and mild flavour. They can crack if over watered

Porter Improved Pink
seedsofchange.com

This indeterminate variety has been specially bred for areas with extreme heat and low humidity and is resistant to cracking and Verticillium and Fusarium Wilt. It produces oval shaped flavoursome pink fruit..

Porter Tomato
reimerseeds.com

Originally produced for Texan conditions, this sweet tasting little tomato variety produces an abundance of deep red, smooth, plum shaped fruit ideal for canning and making juice. Resistant to drought, cracking and sunburn, it is suitable for the hottest of climates, including areas high in humidity.

Purple Calabash
heirloomtomatoplants.com

The Purple Calabash has unusual ruffled purplish black tomato fruits. It has a rich sweet flavour and does well in drought stricken areas.

Thai Red Turtle Egg
rareseeds.com

Tropical tomato variety from Thailand, small red egg- sized fruit have a fine flavour and are great fresh or cooked. This is a very popular variety in the Orient, great for hot climates and wet conditions.

Note: photos kindly provided with the permission of the companies listed alongside each variety. Seeds for these varieties are available from the company listed and in some cases also from other online seed companies - see p88.

Tomato Varieties

There are literally thousands of tomato varieties available throughout the world. Some of them are even the same with different names in different regions! The following tables list some popular varieties as well as some which are a little harder to find. You will need to check what is available in your region at your local nursery or from a seed supplier. Permission to use the photos below was kindly provided by the companies listed alongside each variety. Seeds for these varieties are available from the company listed and in some cases also from other online seed companies - see p88.

Variety		Origin	Season	D / I	Max Yield kg	Max Yield lbs	Size	Shape	Use	Flavour	Comments
Ailsa Craig seeds.thompson-morgan.com			M	I	11.3	25	M	R	T,P	Little	Bred in Scotland back in 1925. A heavy cropper, it can be grown in the greenhouse or outdoors
Amish Paste seedsavers.org		Heir	M	I	15.7	35	M	P	T,P	Lots	Amish heirloom discovered in Wisconsin. Produces 150-200gm (6-8 oz) red fruits that are oxheart to almost teardrop-shaped. Meaty fruits are juicy and have really outstanding flavour. Good for sauce or fresh eating. Indeterminate, 85 days from transplant
Apollo		Hyb	E	D	10.8	24	M	R	R,P	Good	The classic early to fruit variety which means that it will set fruit at around 22°C, whereas a mid season variety needs around 25°C to set fruit. This plant is a tall grower, so pinch out early sideshoots. Two main leaders (branches) should be developed although the plant will cope with more leaders if well fed. If you have more leaders, you usually get more fruit, but slightly smaller.
Aunt Ruby's German Green heirloomtomatoplants.com		Heir	E	I			L	B	T	Good	Big, sweet beefsteaks, bursting with a fragrant, complex, spicy-sweetness with a touch of tang. With its intricate, earthy, unforgettable flavour, this one will broaden your tomato horizons. Very adaptable and easy to grow with good disease resistance.
Azoychka totallytomato.com		Heir	E	I	11.5	25	M	B	T,P	Lots	The Russian Azoychka is regular leaf, quite early, good sized oblate shaped, yellow fruit with bright yellow interiors and a nice tart taste.

Legend. Origin: Heirloom or Hybrid. **Season:** E=Early, M=Main, L=Late, **D/I:** Determinate or Indeterminate, **Size:** S=Small, M=Medium, L=Large, **Shape:** B=Beefsteak, O=Oxheart, P=Paste, R=Round, **Use:** D=Drying, P=Paste, S=Stuffing, T=Table. **Note:** Yield was determined during trials by the Diggers Club in Australia. www.diggers.com.au

www.bestjuicytomatoes.com

16

How to Grow Juicy Tasty Tomatoes

Variety		Origin	Season	D / I	Max Yield kg	Max Yield lbs	Size	Shape	Use	Flavour	Comments
Banana Legs reimerseeds.com		Heir	M	D	9.5	21	S	P	P	Little	This has bright yellow fruit that is 10 cm (4") long x 4cm (1 1/2") in diameter, resembling a small banana. Tomatoes turn yellow when mature. Excellent for brightening up salads or gourmet dishes. Very meaty and suitable for making sauce and paste.
Big Rainbow reimerseeds.com		Heir	L	I	17.8	39	L	B	T,P	Good	Large yellow beefsteak, as the fruits ripen, go through a phase where they resemble a rainbow - 'greenback' on the shoulders, yellow in the middle, and with red blushed pink on the blossom end. The early set fruit can be very large at 900grams (2 lbs) or more. It is relatively free of fruit defects, and bears well. Highly rated in taste tests.
Black Krim roguelands.com			E	I	7.1	16	L	R	T,P	Lots	From Krim on the Black Sea in the former Soviet Union, Black Krim has a superb smoky sweetness with a delicate lingering touch of tang in a 10-15cm (4-6") slightly flattened, mahogany-coloured fruit with lovely, deep green shoulders.
Black Prince roguelands.com		Heir	E	I			S	R	T	Lots	An intensely flavoured rich and juicy, heirloom. Prolific, easy to grow, it fruits in 70 days with clusters of small-medium deep, dark mahogany-red fruits.
Black Russian organiccatalog.com		Heir	E	I	7.4	16	S	R	T,D	Lots	Heavy early producer of medium sized black tomatoes. Fruit is smooth, taste is sweet, spicy and slightly salty. Not to be confused with the Russian Black variety.

Legend. Origin: Heirloom or Hybrid. **Season:** E=Early, M=Main, L=Late, **D/I:** Determinate or Indeterminate. **Size:** S=Small, M=Medium, L=Large, **Shape:** B=Beefsteak, O=Oxheart, P=Paste, R=Round, **Use:** D=Drying, P=Paste, S=Stuffing, T=Table. **Note:** Yield was determined during trials by the Diggers Club in Australia. www.diggers.com.au

Variety		Origin	Season	D / I	Max Yield kg	lbs	Size	Shape	Use	Flavour	Comments
Brandy Wine *roguelands.com*		Heir	E	I	14.1	9	L	B	T,P	Lots	This Amish heirloom packs in the 'real' tomato flavour. Brandywine is well known for its size and exotic, sweet tomato flavour. Open pollinated. Potato leaf plants have a compact indeterminate growth habit which produce large fruit with a pinkish red flesh. Yellow, pink and black cultivars also available.
Broad Ripple Yellow Currant *seedsavers.org*			M	I	5.2	11	S	R	T	Lots	Introduced by Seed Savers Exchange in 1984, 'Broad Ripple Yellow Currant' was originally found growing in a street crack in Indianapolis. This prolific indeterminate will produce hundreds of tiny cherry tomatoes, bursting with flavour, until frost.
Calypso *technisem.com*			M	I	17.7	39	L	O	T,P	Good	Red bush type. Bred for humid tropical areas. Slightly flattened, firm, high yield, good disease resistance.
Celebrity *reimerseeds.com*		Hyb	M	D	18.6	41	L	R	T,P	Little	Celebrity is a superior all-around tomato with great disease resistance. Plant produces high yields of 200gm (8 oz) red tomatoes all season long until frost. Tomatoes are firm and flavourful and turn red when mature. Plant has strong vines and does extremely well in most regions.
Colossal Yellow *victoryseeds.com*		Hyb	L	I	12.7	28	L	B	T	Good	Needs staking to hold the 1.5 to 2 metre (5-6ft) bush upright. The huge pale yellow 10-18cm (4-7 inch) solid deep oblate fruits set in mid season and are low in acid.
Cuatomate *agrestalseeds.com*		Heir	M	I	3.8	8	S	R	T	Good	Medium-sized vining plants produce an ongoing supply of small, round tomatoes less than 1" (2.5cm) in diameter until frost. Skin matures from orange to red. Taste varies between sweet and tart all in one mouthful. Originates from the Zapotec Indians, Oaxaca, Mexico.

Legend. **Origin:** Heirloom or Hybrid, **Season:** E=Early, M=Main, L=Late, **D/I:** Determinate or Indeterminate, **Size:** S=Small, M=Medium, L=Large, **Shape:** B=Beefsteak, O=Oxheart, P=Paste, R=Round, **Use:** D=Drying, P=Paste, S=Stuffing, T=Table. **Note:** Yield was determined during trials by the Diggers Club in Australia. www.diggers.com.au

Variety	Origin	Season	D / I	Max Yield kg	lbs	Size	Shape	Use	Flavour	Comments
Gardeners Delight *gardenandleisure.com*		E	I	9.7	21	S	R	T,P,D	Lots	This vigorous cherry variety produces long trusses of small size fruits which are extremely sweet in flavour. Usually grown outdoors or in containers on the patio.
Glory of Moldova *landrethseeds.com*	Heir	M	I	14.7	32	M	R	T	Good	Prolific and beautiful old heirloom is round, bright carrot-orange salad tomato with mild, delicious, creamy sweet flavour and a little bit of tang in the background. Keeps well after picking and grows on a smaller type plant, up to 1.5m (5 ft).
Gold Nugget *thompson-morgan.com*		E	D	9	20	S	R	T,D	Little	Sweet small golden-yellow globe shaped fruits ripen very early in the season. This small plant is perfectly suited for containers or garden borders and does well in all climates.
Golden Sunburst *seedsbydesign.com*		L	I	13.6	30	S	R	T	Good	Indeterminate vine, excellent quality small golden fruit. Suited for containers or borders.
Great White Beefsteak *roguelands.com*	Heir	L	I			L	B	T	Good	The largest of the white tomato varieties, the Great White produces huge creamy tomatoes that can weigh up to 1 kg (2lbs) and deliver a sweet, juicy flavour. Extremely productive and hardy, the dense foliage protects against sun scald. Drought and crack resistance makes this variety a good choice for hot climates.
Green Zebra *roguelands.com*	Hyb	E	I	13.7	30	S	R	T	Lots	Abundantly productive plant, this 5cm (2 inch) round fruit ripens to a amber gold with green vertical stripes and green flesh. It is crack resistant and has a mild, slightly tangy flavour.
Grosse Lisse *gardenexpress.com.au*		M	I	16.4	36	M	R	T	Good	Vigorous, adapted to humid areas. Large, (plus 200 grams) heavy yielding cultivar. Moderate sweetness, low to moderate acidity. Very popular variety.

Legend. **Origin:** Heirloom or Hybrid, **Season:** E=Early, M=Main, L=Late, **D/I:** Determinate or Indeterminate, **Size:** S=Small, M=Medium, L=Large, **Shape:** B=Beefsteak, O=Oxheart, P=Paste, R=Round, **Use:** D=Drying, P=Paste, S=Stuffing, T=Table. **Note:** Yield was determined during trials by the Diggers Club in Australia. www.diggers.com.au

How to Grow Juicy Tasty Tomatoes

Variety	Origin	Season	D / I	Max Yield (kg)	Max Yield (lbs)	Size	Shape	Use	Flavour	Comments
Ida Gold *seedstrust.com*		E	D	4.1	9	S	R	T	Good	An early determinate and hardy plant which yields a concentrated fruit set of small oblong fruits even under extreme conditions. These attractive orange beauties have a sweet, fruity flavour.
Little Sugar Yellow *diggers.com.au*		M	I	8	18	S	R	T	Good	Tall growing, there are garden designers who climb these up trellis in front of brick or rendered walls. When they fruit, it gives a stunning effect.
Mighty Red *diggers.com.au*	Hyb	M	D	12.9	28	L	B	T,P	Little	A good early grafted tomato which produces an abundance of large, globe shaped fruit of good colour and good tolerance to common tomato diseases. Grafted tomatoes are extremely vigorous and require plenty of space, fertiliser and water to achieve their growth potential.
Mortgage Lifter *roguelands.com*	Heir	M	I	16.4	36	L	B	T,P	Lots	This giant, popular, legendary heirloom from West Virginia, USA, is sweet, juicy, delicious and prolific, with lovely old time tomato flavour. The meaty pink-red fruits weigh between 0.5 to 1.8 kg (1 - 4 lbs)! The plant continues to bear fruit right up until frost and keeps very well. Good producer in drought stricken areas.
Napoli Paste *victoryseeds.com*		M	I	13.7	30	S	P	P	Good	An easy to grow variety with plum shaped fruit. Very popular for tomato paste as well as for canning, juice or puree. Compact plants with some root and stem disease resistance, Napoli produces small 80 gm (3 oz) bright red, pear shaped, solid fruit.
Old Fashioned Red Beefsteak *roguelands.com*		L	I			L	B	T	Good	A large and very popular red tomato with a fine taste and very firm flesh. Used for slicing, using in salads or for canning.

Legend. **Origin:** Heirloom or Hybrid, **Season:** E=Early, M=Main, L=Late, **D/I:** Determinate or Indeterminate, **Size:** S=Small, M=Medium, L=Large, **Shape:** B=Beefsteak, O=Oxheart, P=Paste, R=Round, **Use:** D=Drying, P=Paste, S=Stuffing, T=Table. **Note:** Yield was determined during trials by the Diggers Club in Australia. www.diggers.com.au

Variety	Origin	Season	D / I	Max Yield kg	Max Yield lbs	Size	Shape	Use	Flavour	Comments
Peruvian Sugarlump *diggers.com.au*		M	I	8.6	19	S	R	T,P,D	Lots	An open pollinated indeterminate climbing vine which really needs a 2 metre (2yds) high cylinder of weld mesh to climb over. The 2-5cm (3/4-2") cherry type fruits are very sweet and similar in taste to Gardener's Delight but they set a bit later in the early season.
Pink Cherry *diggers.com.au*		E	I	10.8	24	S	R	T,P,D	Lots	These prolific plants produce 2cm (3/4 inch) round pink cherry tomatoes. Delicious sweet flavour are ideal for snacking or adding great flavour to a salad.
Principe Borghese *roguelands.com*		E	D	2.9	6	S	R	D	Good	Italian variety, a favourite for Sun dried Tomatoes. The small prolific plants produce lots of intensely tasty fruit with a distinctive rich tanginess and very few seeds. In dry climates, the plant, can be hung over a fence in the shade to dry the fruits. Excellent colour and flavour when dehydrated. Dried fruits store well and can be reconstituted in water or olive oil. Plants need support due to hundreds of fruits.
Purple Calabash *cedarknollfarm.com*	Heir	M	I	9	20	B	B	T,P	Lots	May be the most purple of all purple tomatoes; a deep purple/ burgundy, and very colourful! The fruit is flat, ribbed and ruffled. Flavour is intense, sweet and tart, with a lime or citrus taste, almost wine like. The plants give huge yields. Crack resistant and stores well.
Red Cherry *roguelands.com*		E	I	7	15	S	R	T, P, D	Lots	Pinkish-red fruits are oval and have full flavour. Plants are fairly compact and great for home gardens and hanging planters. Great for stir fries, snacking and salads.
Roma *roguelands.com*		E	D			S	P	T,P	Good	This disease resistant variety produces oblong red, plum-like tomatoes of a medium size. Roma is ideal for making tomato paste or for canning.

Legend. Origin: Heirloom or Hybrid, **Season:** E=Early, M=Main, L=Late, **D/I:** Determinate or Indeterminate, **Size:** S=Small, M=Medium, L=Large, **Shape:** B=Beefsteak, O=Oxheart, P=Paste, R=Round, **Use:** D=Drying, P=Paste, S=Stuffing, T=Table. **Note:** Yield was determined during trials by the Diggers Club in Australia. www.diggers.com.au

Variety	Origin	Season	D / I	Max Yield kg	Max Yield lbs	Size	Shape	Use	Flavour	Comments
Rouge de Marmande *oystercoveseeds.com*		E	I	14	31	M	B	T,P	Good	A vigorous French variety with strong flavoured, flattish red tomatoes will set large amounts of fruit even in cool weather. Surround the young plants with lots of straw around the base to keep the ripening tomatoes off the ground.
Rutgers *roguelands.com*	Hyb	E	D			M	R	T,S	Good	Produces intense, red coloured, round tomato fruits are produced on a strong vine. An improved, disease resistant strain. Fruit is 180gm (6 oz), globular, slightly flattened with smooth, thick walls that are crack resistant.
Tigerella *organiccatalog.com*	Heir	E	I	20	44	S	R	T,P	Lots	This wonderful old-time British heirloom tomato bears huge crops of small orange-red round fruits with yellow-orange vertical stripes. A European favourite, the fruits are surprisingly lively: tangy, richly flavoured, very prolific, and one of the most beautiful tomatoes you'll ever see.
Tommy Toe *seedsaversorg.com*	Heir	E	I	11.3	25	S	R	T,P,D	Lots	Heirloom from the Ozark Mountains. Bears loads of deep red fruits with exceptional flavour for fresh eating, salads and juices. Extremely vigorous plant yields hundreds of 2-3cm (1") apricot-sized fruits over an extended season.
Verna Orange *edenseeds.com.au*	Heir	M	I	12.9	28	L	O	T,P	Good	Beautiful orange oxheart shape, early bearing, prolific and tasty, good for sandwiches as fruit won't go mushy.

Legend. **Origin:** Heirloom or Hybrid, **Season:** E=Early, M=Main, L=Late, **D/I:** Determinate or Indeterminate, **Size:** S=Small, M=Medium, L=Large, **Shape:** B=Beefsteak, O=Oxheart, P=Paste, R=Round, **Use:** D=Drying, P=Paste, S=Stuffing, T=Table. **Note:** Yield was determined during trials by the Diggers Club in Australia. www.diggers.com.au

Variety	Origin	Season	D / I	Max Yield kg	Max Yield lbs	Size	Shape	Use	Flavour	Comments
White Beauty reimerseeds.com	Heir	L	I	8.8	19	L	B	T	Good	The whitest of the white tomatoes, White Beauty also has one of the finest flavours among the whites which can sometimes be rather bland. Can reach 450 grams (16 ounces) but is normally in the 280 gram (10 ounce) range. Since the recent rediscovery of the seeds it has become especially popular for its good yield and lovely, creamy, almost seedless fruits.
White Wonder victoryseeds.com		M	I			M	B	T,P	Good	Mild, sweet flavoured with high sugar content. Yellowish-white inside and out when matured. Fruits are sized on bushy, leafy plants. Good for slicing and canning. Even the large sized fruits maintain good texture and flavour.
Yellow Peach seedsofchange.com	Heir	M	I	5.8	13	S	R	P	Good	Fuzzy fruits ripen to yellow and often have a hint of pink blush when fully ripe. Outstanding flavour, rarely cracks. Uniform and productive variety.
Yellow Pear roguelands.com	Heir	L	I			S	R	T	Good	Golden yellow teardrop shaped tiny fruit that has beautiful colour and a sweet burst of flavour. Easy to grow and the first to ripen of the season. This tomato is so vigorous that it is notorious for self seeding. Yellow Pear is also a great cold tolerant tomato variety and will generally last further into the season than other varieties. As the plants themselves are very vigorous, staking or caging is required.
Yellow Plum roguelands.com	Heir	M	I			S	P	T,P	Good	An old open pollinated tomato variety that produces a huge crop of 30-50gm (1-2 ounce) plum shaped yellow tomatoes. They are very similar to traditional red plum tomatoes except for their golden yellow colour. Yellow Plum makes a wonderful paste tomato and can be used for making yellow tomato sauces, salads and canning.

Legend. Origin: Heirloom or Hybrid, **Season:** E=Early, M=Main, L=Late, **D/I:** Determinate or Indeterminate, **Size:** S=Small, M=Medium, L=Large, **Shape:** B=Beefsteak, O=Oxheart, P=Paste, R=Round, **Use:** D=Drying, P=Paste, S=Stuffing, T=Table. **Note:** Yield was determined during trials by the Diggers Club in Australia. www.diggers.com.au

6. Site Preparation

The right site, healthy soil and warm temperatures are crucial for growing tomatoes.

Site Selection

Tomatoes grow in frost free conditions in a warm, sunny spot.

In warm, frost-free zones (for example the tropical and subtropical parts of northern Australia and the southern states in USA (including Hawaii) tomatoes can be grown all year round.

In temperate climates seed can be planted from late winter to early summer providing tomatoes through Summer and into Autumn (Fall).

In cool to cold climates delay planting until early Spring and make last plantings by the end of Spring. Staggering plantings through Spring and early Summer will extend your harvest period.

The reason for Winter culture in the northern tropics and sub-tropics in Australia, South East Asia, Central America and East Africa, is that the tomato is plagued by fungal diseases which are rampant in the humid tropics during the wet Summer. It's only during the Winter dry season that good crops can be produced in the open.

Tomato plants love sun and heat and where possible they should be grown with full exposure. This is particularly important in cool and temperate climates where cool summers frequently occur. Low temperatures, particularly at night, are the principal cause of the failure of the flowers to set fruit.

Extreme temperatures of around 35-40°C (95-105°F) can result in the flowers falling off their buds. Poor fruit set can also be caused by establishing plants in sheltered sites.

Tomatoes are self-pollinating: the flower contains both male and female organs. In most cases tomato flowers are totally closed, so they are limited to self-pollination. Transfer of pollen from male to female organs relies on some form of motion to dislodge pollen so that it falls on the ovary.

Any form of disturbance, or motion such as wind enhances transfer of pollen. If tomato plants are well protected, they can experience flower failure. Always plant tomatoes to take full advantage of the sun for growth and the wind for pollination.

Wind

Tomatoes are relatively tolerant of windy conditions, but the wind will cause staked tomatoes to chafe on the stake and will also increase water loss, unless mulch is used. The most critical stage is from fruit set onwards as tomatoes can be damaged from scuffing between fruit and stems. This causes light brown scabs on the fruit.

Windbreaks will help reduce these problems, but care needs to be taken that the wind breaks do not shade the crop and are far enough away that they do not interfere with the growth of the tomatoes.

Soil Erosion

Whilst a flat site is the best for growing tomatoes, some gardeners may be restricted to use a site with a slope. Steep slopes are often subject to erosion caused by runoff water carrying away the good top soil.

Where tomatoes are to be grown on sites with a slope, a

number of steps may be taken to avoid erosion:

1. Apply mulch around the tomatoes, however don't mulch right against the tomato stems as this might cause stem rot.

2. Plant a band of grass below the tomatoes.

3. Run beds across the slope to minimize loss of soil and increase water infiltration.

4. Dig a contour slope below

Heavy clay soils hold water and can restrict root growth

Sandy soils are often low in nutrients

Rocky soils also restrict root growth and can be lacking in nutrients

A beautiful loamy soil will be full of worms, free draining and contain plenty of nutrients

the tomatoes to catch runoff water and soil.

What makes good soil?

Any farmer will tell you that good soil:

- drains well and warms up quickly in the Spring

- does not crust after planting

- soaks up heavy rains with little runoff

- stores moisture for drought periods

- has few clods and no hardpan

- supports high populations of soil organisms

- has that rich, earthy smell

- produces healthy, high quality crops.

All these criteria indicate a soil that functions effectively today and will continue to produce long into the future.

How to treat soil over Winter

If you live in an area where the soil stays wet and heavy for most of Winter, you can still do things to improve it. For example:

- Don't dig very wet soil and don't walk over it or compact it with vehicles or heavy machinery.

- Drench the soil with a hose-on clay breaker.

- Add layers of organic matter to the surface. This will protect the soil from erosion (from heavy rain) and compaction. It won't break down as fast as in warm weather but it will gradually rot and improve the soil.

- When the soil dries out, a drainage system could be installed to minimise the problem next winter.

Check your soil Type

To check out the soil, you will need to dig several holes (about 30cm deep) in your tomato garden site. This will give you an idea of the soil profile. Pay particular attention to the layers in the soil. A typical garden soil will have a thin layer of top soil over a subsoil where there is not much organic matter. It may be heavy clay, stony, rock, builder's rubble or the soil may be sandy to a great depth - typical in beach-side gardens.

How to improve your soil

All soils used for growing plants will benefit from additional organic matter, but the different particle sizes of various soil types require different solutions.

Clay Soil

Clay soils tend to be have a high plant nutrient content, but they are both difficult to water and easily waterlogged. Clay soils can be improved by cultivating the soil and adding gypsum (clay breaker).

Sandy Soil

Sandy soils usually have excellent drainage and low nutrient levels. They are also susceptible to wind and rain erosion. They can be improved with organic matter.

Rocky Soil

Rocky soils can't be cultivated and are usually very low

in plant nutrients. In this situation the cheapest option may be to build garden beds on top of the existing soil. This can be done by importing soil to the site or by using the No Dig gardening method. Simply build up the soil by laying down layers of organic material such as compost, newspapers and lawn clippings.

Compacted Soils

Because clay soils are made up of very small particles, they can be easily compressed together by the weight of vehicles or pedestrians. This results in soil that either repels water, or once wet, is unable to dry out. It is also low in the oxygen needed by plant roots.

Aerate compacted soils by digging them over and mixing in loose material such as compost or washed sand. Another way is to use an aerating tool that creates holes in the surface; then spread a sandy loam around to fall into those holes. (This technique is used in the turf industry.)

Check your drainage

To check how well your soil drains, fill the holes with water and check how long it takes for the holes to empty. If it drains away very quickly then you

Test your soil to ensure that the pH is around 6.0 - 6.5

probably have sandy soil and moisture retention will be an ongoing problem. Mulching, adding organic material and using water-storing crystals or granules are suitable strategies to use. If the water is still there after a few hours then drainage will be a challenge in your tomato garden. If this is the case you need to consider planting into raised beds or installing drainage.

Ideal soil type for tomatoes

The preferred soil is a sandy loam that is free-draining and easy to work; its water-holding capacity is subsequently improved by adding organic matter.

Tomato roots are capable of penetrating several metres underground which means that the soil should be aerated by double digging with a spade (or deep ripping with a tractor on larger plots). If it is not possible to dig down deep as the soil is compact or has a solid clay barrier, then break up sub-surface layers or create raised beds or do both. Preparing the soil to the right depth will provide suitable drainage conditions for many years to come.

Tomato plants thrive in beds in which a winter green manure has been grown and dug in when it matures. It will be full of worms, which continue to break the organic matter down and vastly improve the soil quality.

Soil pH

Tomatoes prefer a slightly acid soil, around 6.0 to 6.5. Soils with a pH outside of 5-7pH will cause unbalanced growth

due to reduced uptake of nutrients. If the soil pH is less than 6.0 apply lime or dolomite . To raise the soil pH by one increment (e.g.: from 5.0 to 6.0) apply 120 grams (4oz) per square metre (square yard) to a sandy soil and up to 380 grams (13oz) per square metre (square yard) to a heavy clay soil.

To lower your soil pH you need to add agricultural sulphur (try your garden centre). Sandy soil - use 25 grams per square metre Loamy soil - 50-70 grams per square metre Clay soil - 100 grams per square metre These amounts will lower the pH of the top 10cm by about 1 pH unit.

Check the pH of your soil using a pH testing kit. These are readily available from most nurseries and are very easy to use. There are different kinds but the most common involves taking a small soil sample (about 1 teaspoonful) and mixing it with a small amount of a chemical provided, then sprinkling the mixture with the special powder provided. The powder will change colour and you then match the colour of your sample with the colour on the card included in the kit. The card will tell you what the colour means.

Improving soil fertility

Plants need nutrients to grow; and any soil can lose its supply of nutrients over time if you don't replenish them.

The best way to do this is to keep adding compost, manure, or mulch – every year, if not more often. As these materials decompose, they release nutrients, maintaining a high level of soil fertility.

Fertilisers should be used as well, to supplement or top up the plants' nutrient requirements. Don't depend totally on fertiliser though: it just isn't enough in most cases. Inorganic fertilisers can also cause environmental damage when used over long periods.

How do you add organic matter?

The best way to improve any type of soil is to add large amounts or organic material. That is why it is so important to get those compost bins operational. In most areas there are ample quantities of Autumn (Fall) leaves available

Regular additions of compost will keep your soil enriched

Compost bins come in numerous shapes and sizes and are easy to use

If you have the room, make three compost heaps, so that you have one that is always ready to use

for anyone with a rake and a packet of plastic bin liners - just keep filling them up!

If you have access to a mulcher, chop up the leaves (or run over them with the mower) so that they break down quicker. If you haven't, just add them to your garden or compost them. Because they don't smell you can easily compost them in a heap. Just keep turning them over regularly. By the next summer they will have been converted to lovely rich leaf mould.

How to make good compost

You have the choice of using a closed compost bin which prevents rats and other nasties from breeding in the composting material or you can build an open heap. The disadvantage of a bin is that it is more difficult (but not impossible) to get air into the mix, although some commercially available compost bins have vents around each side.

A heap is more untidy, but easier to manage and probably achieves a faster processing of the materials. One of the most popular heap structures is the three stage heap. You only add to one heap at a time, which means that each heap is in a different stage of readiness. You always have one heap ready to use, another one in decomposing state and a third that you're adding to.

Compost that is ready to be applied to the garden does not smell bad, but has a sweet, earthy smell. Always use gardening gloves when handling compost and other organic materials.

Begin by checking that the compost bin that you are making or have purchased is open at the top and open at the bottom.

The top will need a tight fitting lid and the bottom should be in direct contact with the soil, in a well-drained area of your backyard.

Place a 10-15cm layer of twigs inside your bin to start off with as this will help to circulate air through your compost as it decomposes.

Now it is time to feed your compost bin! The types of organic matter that can go into your compost bin fall under two categories — 'greens' and 'browns'.

Greens are organic matter that are high in nitrogen and are living matter, such as vegetable scraps, green garden waste, manure, etc.

Browns are organic matter that are high in carbon and are non-living matter, such as dead, dried leaves, sawdust, dead grasses, twigs, straw, etc.

It is important that you balance the amount of greens and browns that go into the compost bin for proper decomposition and to create healthier compost.

Begin by making alternative layers of greens and browns in your compost bin, on top of the twigs. Start with the greens and make two different layers of greens. Next make two different layers of browns. Finish off with a layer of good quality soil or compost.

Once this layering is complete, secure the lid on your compost bin to retain the heat and protect it from the sun and rain. Continue to create the layers of greens or browns in your compost bin and top off with a layer of good quality soil or compost. Always remember to secure the lid on your compost when you have finished feeding it.

Tips on Composting

Locate your bin or heaps in a semi-shaded area of the garden. The material in the bin will get hot as it decomposes, but after the hot stage you want earthworms to colonise the compost. A bin in the sun may be too hot for earthworms.

Don't put weeds with seed heads and invasive plants that strike easily from stem tissue in the bin or heap. A really hot compost heap can kill these off, but you would need a very big heap and the outside of the heap would have to be turned to the inside in order to kill all the material.

Chop up everything as small as you can. Run the mower over leaves, put prunings through a mulcher or chop them manually. This greatly increase the rate of decomposition.

Add vegetable scraps, shredded newspaper and fallen leaves to your compost heap

Keep the mixture moist: too wet and there will not be enough air, too dry and decomposition will slow down dramatically.

Get air into the mixture by turning it over regularly. Bins with ridges down the side and revolving bins are helpful in aerating compost. Without enough air the mix becomes anaerobic - it really stinks and can become so acidic that it can kill plants. A broomstick can be used effectively to fluff up material in a closed bin (even pushing a stick down into the compost to make "breathing holes" works well).

Decomposition relies on lots of microbes. The material you put in the compost bin will contain plenty, but to give the population a boost, add a shovelful of compost from the last batch, or a shovelful of soil.

Adding lime may reduce the smell and speed up decomposition but can cause a loss of nitrogen. Adding some gypsum will provide additional calcium and it also helps to reduce the smell.

Don't include meat and fats in your composting materials, or citrus skins and onions which earthworms hate.

It is a good idea to have two bins or heaps - one that you are adding to daily and one that is "cooking" - it takes several months for compost to be ready for use.

Mulching

Mulching tomatoes is also strongly recommended, not only to inhibit weed growth but over the long term it will provide nutrients to the bed and improve soil structure.

At the onset of hot weather mulching will shade the soil and aid in retaining soil moisture. Cool and moist soil provides the ideal conditions for earthworms to burrow which improves air porosity and enhances organic content. Be sure to saturate the soil after applying the mulch, or it can act as a barrier to the penetration of moisture.

It is important not to apply mulch too early in Spring, or the warming rays of sunshine will not reach the soil because the protective cover of the mulch will have the effect of reducing growth.

Summary of mulching benefits:

- Mulching reduces evaporation. This means that less watering is necessary. This saves time, money and is environmentally desirable. It is particularly valuable in areas where soil salinity is high.

- Mulching keeps soil temperatures cooler. (An exception to this is the use of black plastic as a mulch which is undesirable for a number of reasons and particularly because it increases soil temperatures to such high levels in summer that roots can be destroyed.)

- The use of organic mulches means that the soil will benefit from the addition of nutrients as the mulch decomposes. Mulches attract earthworms which add to the health of the soil through aeration and provide readily available nutrients for plants in the form of worm casts.

- Because mulching protects the soil surface from the compacting effect of rain and

Mulch covers

Straw mulch

Pine bark mulch

Red plastic mulch

sprinklers which can cause crusting, it allows the soil to absorb water more readily and prevents excessive run off. This can also help prevent erosion.

- Mulching helps to maintain good soil structure. This means that your plant's roots have maximum access to moisture and oxygen.

- Mulching is an effective and environmentally friendly way of achieving weed control.

Tips to help you make the best decisions about mulch for your garden.

- Pine bark appears to control the growth of some pathogenic fungi that can damage plants.

- Bark chip mulch (particularly if it is fresh) can deplete the soil's nitrogen supplies as nitrogen is used up in decomposition. Add extra nitrogen.

- Lawn clippings need to be thoroughly dried before using as a mulch, otherwise the material can form a waterproof crust. Mix them with leaf mould or compost them.

- Mushroom compost is often quite alkaline and is better off being added to your compost

- Pea straw adds nitrogen to the soil. When you use it, pea plants invariably pop up and these can be dug in to the soil. This is called a "green manure" crop.

- Layers of paper are often used under mulch as a weed suppressant but this may attract nematodes. Thick layers of paper can also be colonised by termites.

- Black plastic suppresses weeds but it can lead to oxygen depletion, inadequate watering and root damage.

- Water well before applying mulch.

- Mulch should not be applied any thicker than 75mm (3 inches). Fine mulch should be applied more thinly e.g.: 40mm (1 1/2 inches); coarser material can be applied more thickly. Mulch that is too thick causes deoxygenation which can kill your plants.

- The use of plastic mulches has also become popular with some growers. Apparently, red reflected on plants "fools" them into believing they are overcrowded; they will then grow more vigorously. Red also promotes photosynthesis. It only works when an area of red plastic covers an open area of about 1.2 metres (4 feet) on each side of the plants. The average increase in production has been reported to be between 10% to 20%. Put the plastic mulch down in the area where you want to grow tomatoes (full sun, of course) and then cut a small hole for each tomato plant.

- One of the disadvantages of plastic mulch is that it prevents rain from penetrating into the soil which means you may have to irrigate. It may also heat up the soil too much in hot areas, so an ideal mix would be to use the red plastic mulch in spring, than as the weather heats up in summer remove the plastic mulch and replace with organic mulch.

29

Living mulches

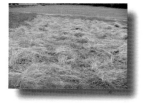

Clover

Vetch

Alfalfa

Living mulch

The Australian CSIRO advises that intensive cultivation and over use of water and chemicals is not sustainable. The use of a self-sustaining crop rotation like Clever Clover works as follows:

- In Autumn (Fall), sow subterranean clover to smother weeds, improve soil-conserving moisture and save on fertilisers. The clover dies down in late spring, and the area is ready for planting summer crops into aerated weed-free soil.

- In Spring, sow alfalfa to draw up water and nutrients from deep down, just like a tree. The alfalfa can be cut every six weeks to provide a summer mulch and slow release fertiliser for tomatoes and other vegetable crops.

The vetch system has been around for decades among farmers practising environment-friendly agriculture. The hairy vetch, a member of the bean family is grown during Winter and mown in the Spring. Farmers set out tomato plants in the matted vetch, which discourages weeds and boosts nitrogen to the soil. It is said to dramatically boost tomato production.

Crop rotation

Tomatoes belong to the same family as potatoes, egg fruit and capsicums. Hence they are subject to the same pests and diseases.

To avoid disease build-up which will affect your tomatoes, it is not recommended that tomatoes be grown on the same patch where related crops have grown for at least three years or indeed where tomatoes have grown within the past three years.

Preparing commercial plots

The following table suggests a land preparation schedule based on the number of weeks before planting:

Weeks before planting	Preparation required
20	If planting a green manure crop, do so at this stage
10 - 12	Slash and/or cut and mulch manure crop
9	Take soil samples
7 - 8	Incorporate green crop as well as lime, dolomite or gypsum where necessary
4	If using a green mulch, disc once to speed break down
1 - 2	Rip or make beds
0	Plant the crop

Initial Cultivation

If the land is covered with grass or weeds, slash, then plough or disc the block. Check for hard pans and a compaction layer (which is usually caused by continual cultivation or traffic). If a pan exists, it may reduce plant growth and can also on occasion cause waterlogging. Deep rip in both directions to break the pan. This is best done when the soil is neither too moist nor too dry. If the soil is too moist, the pan will not shatter, and if the soil is too dry, large clods will form.

Ideally ripping is best done after the previous crop so that any rain that falls has time to penetrate the profile, taking with it any accumulated salts.

Organic additives

With green crops, organic matter is best applied prior to planting of the green crop.

Green manure crops

Building up the soil organic matter is important for any crop, but particularly for tomato crops and especially in light or sandy soils. Legumes such as cowpea and dolichos which are susceptible to nematodes should not be used as cover crops in plots where tomatoes are to be grown.

Soil tests

Soil tests are essential to the good management of a crop, especially high value crops such as tomatoes. Samples should be taken 6 – 8 weeks prior to the intended planting date. This should give adequate time for any soil adjustments to be made. Ideally, lime, dolomite or gypsum should be applied at least a year prior to using the block for tomatoes because it takes considerable time to break down.

Final preparation

Organic matter needs to be incorporated 20 – 25cm (8 – 10 inches) deep and the soil cultivated to a planting tilth. Incorporation must take place well before planting so that it has time to completely decompose otherwise the new tomato crop will be predisposed to damping off diseases. Decomposition times vary: in warm, moist soils this takes about four weeks and in cold, dry soils about eight weeks.

Cultivation of soils with newly applied organic matter often has to take place twice with the latter cultivation required to get the tilth into a clod-free state. After making the beds and fertilizing, a rotary hoe should be used to finish the beds.

Trace elements

As nearly all soils are zinc deficient, zinc sulphate or zinc oxide can be applied at about 20kg/ha (66 lb/acre) or – oxide rate as a pre-plant spray. These should be applied and worked into the top soil at least three weeks before planting.

Solubor (containing boron) can also be applied as a pre-plant spray at 2 – 5kg/ha (6 – 16 lb / acre). Do not apply in combination with the zinc.

Deficiency is most likely in sandy soils, particularly if heavily limed, low in nitrogen or alkaline. Under these circumstances apply commercial liquid preparations for foliar application. These are available for any trace element and work very well.

Table 1: Guide to the amount of lime or dolomite required to raise soil pH to about 6.5

Soil type pH range	Sandy/loam t/ha	Loam t/ha	Clay loam t/ha
4.5 – 5.0	5.00	6.25	7.50
5.0 – 5.5	2.50	3.75	5.00
5.5 – 6.0	1.25	2.50	3.75

Gypsum is used to increase soil calcium levels. It does not change the pH of the soil. It can also be used to ameliorate the effects of sodium in the soil and improve the structure.

Table 2: Guide to the management of calcium, magnesium and pH

Recommended Action	Application rate		Soil nutrient status							
			pH high				pH low			
			Calcium high		Calcium low		Calcium high		Calcium low	
	per hectare (metric)	per acre (imperial)	Mg high	Mg low	Mg high	Mg low	Mg high	Mg low	Mg high	Mg low
Gypsum	1 – 2t	0.44-0.89t			x	x				
Dolomite	2.5 – 5t	1.1-2.2t						x		x
Lime	2.5 – 5t	1.1-2.2t					x		x	
Magnesium sulphate	100-250kg	220-550 lb		x		x	x			

Source for Tables 1 and 2: Queensland Department of Primary Industry

Preparing pots

Any container that is at least 30cm (12 inches) deep and 18 litres (five gallons) in volume is ideal for planting tomatoes. Be sure the container has holes in the bottom for proper drainage. Panty hose or coffee filters come in handy for lining the pot, keeping soil in its place and retaining the moisture that tomato plants love. This method of growing tomatoes is obviously useful for people without a yard or garden plot, but it is also a great way to decorate a patio for the summer.

Regular potting soil works well for tomatoes in small pots and planters. When using a large container, use a soil-less growing mix since it retains the moisture tomatoes love. You can use garden soil as long as you mix in some peat moss, vermiculite or Perlite to improve drainage. Tomatoes need six to eight hours of light, so be sure to put your containers in sunny locations, and if need be, move them as the sun changes position.

While tomatoes are generally attached to stakes, in pots tomatoes can simply hang over the side if you prefer. When transplanting your tomato plants, place the plant in the pot so that the bottom set of leaves is just above the dirt. You'll need to water often as the roots cannot reach for more water as they can in a garden plot. This means that you will probably be watering them once a day during the hottest part of the summer

Make sure you place them in a spot where they'll receive maximum sunlight. If the pots can be placed against the side of the house, a fence or out-building, the heat from the reflected sunlight will be of great benefit in early ripening of the fruit.

Growing conditions in a container can never match those of the ground: roots can spread more widely and deeply in the ground and the soil retains more warmth. Both of these factors promote greater fruit production and greater fruit size on tomato plants.

Fill the container with a soil mix that is equal parts potting soil, perlite, sphagnum peat moss, and compost. Add slow release fertiliser to the mix in amounts recommended on the label. Purchase healthy plants with straight stems that are as thick as a pencil and have at least two to three sets of true leaves. Plant the tomato deeply, with soil up to its first set of true leaves. This will encourage it to grow roots all along the buried stem. Water regularly and begin fertilizing with a water soluble 20-20-20 or 15-30-15 fertilizer once a week after the first fruits appear. Harvest mature fruits regularly to encourage more production.

In addition to following these growing tips, buy tomato varieties that are known to do well in containers. Large tomato varieties include 'Bragger', 'Brandywine', 'Celebrity', 'Delicious', 'Early Girl', 'Fantastic', 'Floradel', 'Husky Gold', 'Oregon Spring', 'Stupice' and 'Walter'. For small and cherry tomatoes, try 'Micro Tom', 'Patio', 'Saladette', 'Small Fry', 'Spring Giant', 'Sungold', 'Summer Cherry', 'Supersweet 100', 'Sweet Million', 'Tiny Tim', 'Toy Boy', 'Tumbler', 'Tumbling Tom', 'Whippersnapper' and 'Yellow Pear'.

Cherry tomatoes grow well in hanging baskets

"Upside down" pots are available from speciality garden stores

Larger varieties will benefit from being staked in larger pots

7. Cultivation

Cultivating your plants involves germinating the seeds, transplanting, staking and pruning.

Jiffy pots

Rockwool cubes

Rockwool little cubes

Peat pots

Sowing Seeds

Raising seedlings indoors or in a controlled climate greenhouse shortens the growing time and improves the germination rate. The minimum temperature for tomato seedlings is 15-29°C (60-84°F). Although they will germinate at 10°C (50°F), they will take around 43 days to germinate rather than the normal eight.

One way to give your seedlings a strong start is to sow seeds into compressed peat pots. These swell in just ten minutes when soaked with water. Alternatively use single cell pots containing seedling mix. These stop roots entangling, something which can happen in seedling punnets.

If you prefer to make up your own seedling mix instead of purchasing a commercial mix, use a combination of compost, potting mix, composted manure and coco peat. Mix it well to

Germination improves in a greenhouse

Mass seedlings in trays

Note the cold stressed seedling on the right

ensure the soil is crumbly and contains no large sods. The baby roots need a soft, well aerated mix in order for them to penetrate and grow well. The healthier the root system, the healthier your plant.

Sow the seeds in this mix and just cover with a little of the mix. Water in with a fine mist or spray. Some sort of cover like a sheet of glass, a clear plastic lid or green house fabric is a good idea. This helps to keep the evaporation down so that the seeds don't dry out while germinating.

Make sure it is warm enough for the germination process. The soil needs to be approximately 20°C for the seeds to germinate, so don't sow them too early! (Seeds may also be sown directly into the soil where they are to grow, but the soil needs to be warm enough.)

After four to six weeks, when seeds are at the four leaf stage, they are ready for hardening off by exposing them to outside temperatures for seven days prior to planting in final position.

Time your seed sowing by checking optimum growing temperatures. This way the emergent seedlings are sown about four to six weeks before your target planting date.

Transplanting

For transplanting to be successful, the soil must be above 15°C (60°F) and there must be no risk of frost. Check soil temperature regularly with a soil thermometer.

Frosts influence the success of transplants, because any reasonable frost is likely to kill the seedlings. This is

The Wall of Water enables you to plant out tomatoes 6-8 weeks earlier than usual inside these protective walls! Plastic water filled tubes absorb heat during the day, release it at night.

Tomato seedlings at true leaf stage, ready for transplanting

Troughing is good for colder areas

Wide spacing provides for good air circulation which reduces potential for disease

particularly a risk in inland areas that have bright spring days where soil temperatures rise to suitable levels, but nights can turn frosty. One technique used in inland areas is to place protective polythene covers, similar to those used by strawberry growers over the seedlings during the first two or three weeks to warm them and protect them from unexpected frosts. Care does need to be taken when the days get hot as the plants can be burnt under them.

When the soil is warm enough and there are no frosts, the plants will grow and eventually produce flowers.

Dipping your seedling plug into a solution of seaweed will boost root growth. When planting, strip lower leaves. Bury the root and most of the bare stem straight, 5 cm (2 inches) under in the garden soil. This will stimulate the growth of the roots.

Troughing is the practice of removing all but the top tuft of leaves of a seedling then digging a shallow trench to plant in. The seedling is laid on its side in the trench about 5-8cm (2 or 3 inches) deep. Its main advantage is in areas with extended cold Springs or very low rainfall.

The plant should be oriented north to south with the root end to the south. The combination of large rooting surface and relatively small leaf area reduces or eliminates transplant shock. Solar heat easily penetrates to the root depth which encourages growth. Overall, it is one of the best planting methods around for tomatoes especially if the seedlings are leggy to begin with.

Spacing

Spacing is partly determined by plant support and pruning. Most people plant tomatoes too close together which generally reduces production.

Staked indeterminates can be grown with spacing of 30cm (1 foot) between plants, caged indeterminates can be grown with spacing of 60 cm (2 feet) between plants, and for sprawling, you need about a 1 metre (1 yard) between plants. The larger the space the more productive they will be.

Determinates can be planted a bit closer than indeterminates especially if they are left to sprawl. They will produce well with 60 cm (2 feet) between plants and 1 metre (1 yard) between rows.

The dwarf varieties are suitable for pot culture but if grown in soil, they can be planted as close as 30 cm (1 foot) apart.

A major contributor to the spacing question is the area of soil the roots expand into. A large tomato plant may have roots 1 metre (1 yard) or more deep and up to 3 metres (10 feet) spread from the plant stem, occupying up to 300 cubic feet of soil.

With trellises, it is advisable to transplant seedlings at least one metre (one yard) apart.

Whatever method of support is used for the plants, it should be constructed soon after transplanting so that any soil disturbance occurs prior to the establishment of the root system.

How to Grow Juicy Tasty Tomatoes

Management and Staking

Once the transplants are established you need to support and train the plants, unless you are growing the dwarf varieties. Professional farmers regularly grow their plants without any support, sprawled across the ground as it is difficult to machine-harvest trellised plants. These varieties however are usually for canning. You can do this in your garden, but they will take up considerable space and look untidy. Fruit and leaves in contact with the soil could be prone to disease.

Traditionally tomato plants are supported either side on a stake or on a trellis with the plants trained to grow into the support by removing some of the branches. Pruning your tomato plants can increase fruit size or improve yield. However some trials have proven that the greater the pruning, the lower the yield of fruit per plant. Pruning did not have any effect on the size of fruit. Different growers will have varied results.

Growing deep, extensive roots and a full leaf canopy will help establish newly transplanted tomatoes. Many experienced tomato growers pull off the first flowers, so the plant does not devote energy to forming fruit before its roots and foliage have filled out. Some gardeners pull off all the flowers and suckers until the plants reach at least 30cm (1 foot) tall.

The following comparison of staking alternatives was undertaken by the U.C. Cooperative Extension, Master Gardener Program, Santa Clara County in USA.

www.mastergardeners.org/picks/tomato_staking.html

Comparison of various staking methods

Wire Mesh Cages	
This method is composed of a series of reinforced cement wire mesh cylinders of graduated diameters. Cages are held together by bending over cut ends or tying with wire. Each cage can be anchored at its base by either a wooden stake, metal rod, t-stake or rebar including by cutting the cage's horizontal wires and pushing remaining vertical wires into ground.	

Advantages	Disadvantages
• Can be stacked inside one another for improved storage space efficiency • All materials can be used for multiple seasons • Easy to work with once made	• Hard to see/collect fruit inside cage due to foliage if plant is not pruned • With taller 7-foot cage sizes, it is difficult to reach top fruit without a ladder • Mesh material rusts which doesn't really matter • May require two or more people to handle the mesh during initial construction

Tools needed	
• Heavy-duty wire cutters	

Cement Reinforcing Mesh Trellis with Conduit

The materials for this method feature a very strong wire mesh of the type used to reinforce cement. Cut lengths of "EMT" electrical conduit support this. In order to demonstrate the ability to build trellis structures appropriate to several heights of vine growths, a stairstep arrangement of three 3 metre (10-foot) wide 1.5 metre (5-foot), 1.8 metre (6-foot), and 2 metre (7-foot) tall sections was constructed prior to planting. These sections were butted end-to-end in a straight line down the middle of a 9 metre (30-foot) row of seedlings.

Each section consisted of the following: a single horizontal 3 metre (10-foot) conduit piece supported by two vertical pieces long enough to be driven 45 to 60 cm (18" to 24") into the ground while still maintaining the requisite above-ground height. The horizontal bar of each section was attached to the two vertical supports with two 45 cm (18-inch) lengths of conduit, bent at right angles using a conduit bender, and inserted into openings of the ends of the three conduit pieces to be joined.

Lastly, a single piece of the mesh was cut so as to fit the 9 metre (30-foot) long, stairstepped conduit framework but extending 15cm (6") above each of the sections. The mesh piece was modified at the shortest end by removing a 30cm x 3 metre (1-foot by 10-foot) section at ground level to facilitate access to the bottoms of the vines. It was attached to pieces to be joined, then attached to the framework using heavy metal wire clips on the crossbars and a lighter wire on the vertical supports. Flatten bottom of vertical posts prior to installation.

Advantages:	Disadvantages
• Cutaway bottom section afforded easier access to work at ground level	• May require two or more people to handle the mesh
• Easy to dismantle and store, either by hanging on fence or wall or rolling	• The cut mesh edges are sharp
• Easy access to fruit and easy to weed around	• Mesh will rust
• Tomato vine snakes through mesh easily	
• Conduit and mesh sections can be used for multiple seasons	
• Uses less wire than cages when plants are closer than six-feet apart in rows with minimum spacing between rows	

Tools needed	Recommendation
• Wire cutters	• Install trellis structure prior to planting
• Saw to cut conduit	
• Sledge hammer or other tool to pound conduit into ground	
• Conduit bender	

Electrical Conduit and Vertical String Method

Similar set up to Cement Reinforcing Mesh with EMT Electrical Conduit Method; however substituting the wire mesh with twine. Cut lengths of natural fibre twine (heavy gauge) and tie a bowline knot at bottom of main young tomato stems when plants begin to sprawl. Twirl the twine around the stems to top of plants in approximately 3 cycles. Tie the excess twine to the horizontal conduit using a clove hitch with a slipknot so it can easily be untied in order to gather more of the plant stems as they grow.

Advantages	Disadvantages
• Fruit easily accessible	• Need to continuously monitor and tie existing and new main plant stem growth
• Workers can access the entire plant	
• Easy to weed	
• Conduit sections easy to store and reuse	

Tools needed	Recommendations
• Wire cutters and twine cutters	Install trellis structure prior to planting
• Saw to cut conduit	
• Sledge hammer or other tool to pound conduit into ground	
• Conduit bender	

Post and Twine Method

This method features 2.4 metre (8-foot) long, 5 cm (2-inch) diameter posts driven into the ground at 3 metre (10-foot) intervals and connected by several horizontally strung rows of natural fibre twine (heavy gauge). A key feature of this method is to "sandwich" the tomato plant between a double-wrap of the twine around each pair of posts. That is, begin and end the first run of the twine on the same side of each post and each plant to be supported. Then string the twine on the opposite side after rounding the second post. The first row of twine is strung about 30 cm (12-inches) above the ground and then continued at no more than 25cm (10-inch) increments as the plant grows.

Advantages	Disadvantages
• Wooden posts can be used for multiple seasons	• Requires continuous twining throughout the season to capture growth
• Easy and space-saving storage	• Twine stretches with the weight of the tomato plant, causing sagging
• Less expensive	• Tends to allow tomato plant to sprawl
	• Needs constant monitoring and working
	• Prone to breakage due to twine breakage/stress on wooden posts
	• May be difficult to remove wooden posts from ground without damage
	• Requires much pruning of plant to optimize this method

Tools needed	Recommendations
• Scissors	• Place posts at 1.2-1.8 metre (4-6 foot) intervals with no more than two plants between posts. This will reduce the stress on the twine from heavy stem and foliage growth.
• Sledge hammer or other tool to pound posts into ground	• Use heavy nylon twine instead of natural jute

Commercial Round Generic Tomato Cage

Lightweight metal, 1 metre (3 feet) tall round cages, with protruding legs that are pushed into the ground.

Advantages	Disadvantages
• Inexpensive	• Difficult to reuse from one season to the next due to bending and/or breaking of wire
	• Requires cages to be reinforced so tomato plants don't cause them to fall over.
	• Plants typically exceed cage height, which either requires extensive pruning or if left unpruned causes stems without support to bend and break.
	• Not strong enough for robust plants

Tools needed	Recommendations
	• Use for "determinate" varieties of tomatoes

Texas Giant Tomato Cages

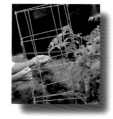

Round galvanized commercial cages which measure 1.5 metres (5 feet) in height with a 60cm (2 foot) diameter and mesh openings which measure 20 x 40cm (8 x 16").

Advantages	Disadvantages
• Come in two sections that fold flat for easy efficient storage	• Expensive
• Strong enough that no staking is required	• 1.5 metre (5-foot) height limitation
• Openings large enough to pick fruit and work plant	• Not widely available
• Does not rust	
• Can be used for multiple seasons	

Square Commercial Tomato Cages

Similar to Round Commercial Tomato Cages but store flat.

Advantages	Disadvantages
• More suitable for determinate varieties	• Plants typically exceed cage height, which cause upper stems to bend and break
	• Cage can tip and cause plant breakage
	• Not strong enough for robust plants

Metal Spiral Rod

Uses a 1.5 metre (5-foot) tall galvanized metal spiral rod which stems are wound around and up. Plants must be pruned to single stems for optimum effectiveness.

Advantages	Disadvantages
• Suitable for tomato plants pruned to one main stem • Can be reused over multiple seasons	• Far too light weight of a support for indeterminant tomatoes • You have to prune off 90% of the plant for it to properly support what is left • Requires reinforcing stake when used for larger plants • Not strong enough for robust sprawling plants • Not readily available

Square Wooden Cage

This method features four wooden 2" x 2", 8-foot tall stakes arranged at 4 corners of a square pattern. Twenty-eight mutually orthogonal holes are drilled at 6-inch intervals beginning at 12" from the ground. Thin rods (such as bamboo or dowels) are inserted into the holes between adjacent posts such that alternating parallel sides of the "square" have two parallel rods every 6 inches along their height. For robust plants, space posts at least 2 1/2-feet apart.

Advantages	Disadvantages
• Excellent way to handle large plants gracefully • Creates eye pleasing garden structure • Minimum pruning required • Rods can be easily removed and re-inserted to capture sprawling plant • Storage areas minimum for stakes and rods	• Initial setup is labour intensive and expensive • May be difficult to see/ pick fruit inside "square"

Tools needed	Recommendations
• Sledge hammer or other tool (recommend pole pounder) to pound stakes into ground • Drill	Install trellis structure prior to planting

Traditional One Stake Method

This method features a stake 1.8-2.4 metre (6-8 foot) tall, which is used to tie tomato stems to. Requires pruning out all but about three main stems.

Advantages	Disadvantages
• Fruit easily accessible • Can plant many varieties in small area as spacing can be as close as 45cm (18") • Access to entire plant • Easy to weed • Minimum materials needed • Stakes reusable and easy to store	• Constant pruning is required • Plant can exceed stake height causing stems to bend and break • Reduces production

Tools needed	Recommendations
• Sledge hammer or other tool (recommend pole pounder) to pound stakes into ground • Ties such as green or clear nursery tape	• Install trellis structure prior to planting • Keep tomato plant pruned to 1 – 3 stems

V-Shaped Stand

This 1.2 metre (4-foot) above ground stand is a heavy gauge wire, prefabricated commercial tomato stand that is in the shape of an open V. Plants grow up into this open V-shape space. Mesh openings in stand allow the tomato vines to snake through.

Advantages	Disadvantages
• More suitable for semi-determinate tomato varieties • Can be used for multiple seasons	• Too short for indeterminants • V-shape space is too small for robust and sprawling plants • Doesn't contain stems, but they tend to fall out on open part of V. • Requires constant pruning to keep vines within V-shape opening • May require additional staking for heavy stem/foliage varieties

Tools Needed	Recommendations
	Use for varieties that are heavily pruned

Pruning your plants

With tomatoes it is important to maximise the efficiency of photosynthesis and limit the amount of disease. To do this the plant needs lots of light and airflow around it.

If a plant is properly pruned and supported, nearly every leaf will have access to the sun. Most of the nutrients and sugars produced are directed towards the newly developing fruit as well as the growing tip. Fruit production does not stop (unless the plant is affected by weather or is lacking in water). As more and more growing tips are produced, via branches, so the plants resources become more divided. This results in ever decreasing fruit size in indeterminate tomato varieties. Determinate varieties are self limiting mainly because of their shorter growing season and more defined fruit setting period.

Those varieties that mature in less than 70 days normally do not require pruning. However, late-season indeterminate varieties often need some of their side shoots or their tops trimmed to prevent them becoming too bushy or tall. With both determinate and indeterminate varieties, it is best to limit the number of trusses to six or seven in order to get good quality fruit.

Pruning also increases plant health. The leaves of a pruned and supported plant dry off faster so that fungal and bacterial diseases have less opportunity to spread.

Essentially, staked and pruned plants have fewer problems with fruit rots and leaf spots because their leaves stay drier, and the plant has good airflow around it. Leaves and fruit should never be allowed to sit on the soil.

How to prune

As the plant grows, suckers appear sequentially from the bottom of the plant up. The farther up the plant a sucker develops, the weaker it is. The reason for this is that the sugar concentration gets lower going up the plant. This means that the suckers that arise from below the first flower cluster, although stronger, affect the strength of the main stem.

If you have a multi-stemmed tomato variety, your aim should be to have all the stems roughly the same size. To do this, keep the tomato plant free of side stems below the first cluster. This will help to create a strong main stem. Then let a second stem grow from the first node above the first fruit. Allow a third stem to develop from the second node above the first set fruit and so forth. Ensuring the stem division is kept as close to the first fruit as possible means those side stems will remain vigorous but will not overwhelm the main stem.

For a strong single vine, remove all suckers and do not stake the plant until the first flowers appear.

Determinate tomato varieties need no pruning other than removal of all suckers below the first flower cluster. Pruning will not affect their vigour or fruit size and in fact will only result in throwing away potential fruit.

Indeterminate tomato plants can have one or many stems, although it is best not to have

Pruning is minimal when you train an indeterminate as a climber.

Pinching out side shoots promotes stronger growth and improves plant health

Small fruits on this cluster should be removed to leave three or four uniform-sized tomatoes

more than four. The fewer the stems, the less space the plant takes up in the garden, and the fewer but larger the fruit as a result of the plant's energy being channelled into flower and fruit production instead of vegetative growth.

Indeterminate tomato varieties are pruned by pinching out the side shoots i.e.: those that appear in the leaf axil. This helps to keep the plant's energy channelled into flower and fruit production instead of vegetative growth. If these side shoots are allowed to grow they will produce a mass of foliage but few tomatoes.

Once six or seven trusses have been formed, stop the plant by trimming off the growing point. If more trusses start to develop, pinch them out to encourage the plant to produce good quality rather than an abundance of poor quality, late-maturing fruit. This final pruning can make all the difference between hard, green fruits and lovely, ripe, juicy fruit.

Also trim off any yellow or spotted leaves in order to reduce the spread of the spot or disease on the plant and its neighbours.

Simple Pruning System

We have already dealt with the 'simple' system which is that where the shoot appearing in the leaf axil is pinched out. This should be done when the shoot is still small and succulent. The base of the shoot, if small enough, can easily be pinched out with the thumb and forefinger. Sometimes if the shoot is a bit longer, it may be necessary to bend it back and forth in order to break it. The sucker should break off leaving a small wound

that should quickly heal. Do not prune prior to a period of rain which might facilitate the entry of bacteria to the fresh wound. Avoid cutting with a knife or scissors unless the shoot is too tough to break off or unless the tools are sterilised between plants. (This can be done using a 10% solution of bleach – sodium hypochlorite).

Missouri Pruning System

In this method, instead of cutting off the whole shoot in the leaf axil, only the growing point is cut off. This causes the shoot stem to divide into two new growing shoots.

This system is best employed when suckers have become too large to chop out next to the main stem (in case disease sets in). This system is also not as much of a shock to the plant as is removing 30cm (1 foot) or so of stem. There is also an advantage and that is that the plant has more leaf area for photosynthesis and because of this, the fruit are less likely to be scorched by the sun. This has to be balanced against the increased disease risk.

In summer, suckers can grow very quickly. However, as these side stems are generally less thrifty than the main stems and tend to produce inferior fruit, it is best to get rid of them.

Removing old leaves from the lower part of the plant improves air movement under the plants. Leaf removal should result in clean, smooth stem scars

Plastic clip holding plant stem on trellis string

Photos in this pruning section sourced from University of Florida, Institute of Food and Agricultural Sciences Florida Greenhouse Vegetable Production Handbook- Volume 3, rev 2001. http://edis.ifas.ufl.edu/CV247

8. Watering your plants

Too much or too little water can cause disease and retard growth. So how much is enough?

Using sprinklers to water tomatoes can increase the likelihood of fungal diseases

Drip irrigation provides water near the base of the plants, leaving upper foliage dry and less susceptible to fungal diseases.

Tomatoes require an even supply of water throughout the season as an irregular water supply will cause your tomatoes to develop problems.

Water absorbed by roots makes its way to the leaves where some of the water molecules are split during photosynthesis, releasing oxygen and energy. Water not used in photosynthesis cools leaves in a process known as transpiration.

Drought stressed tomato plants will be smaller with fewer fruit and more likely to succumb to disease and insects. Gardeners know that blossom-end rot increases with dry soils.

When water is applied to the soil, there are a variety of things that can happen. If too much is applied, some may runoff and never soak into the ground. This results in erosion and is certainly something we need to avoid. Some evaporates off the surface of the soil (and the surface of the leaves). How much depends on the temperature, humidity, and air movement.

A sunny, dry, day with a bit of wind will result in much more evaporation than a cloudy, cool day. How fast the water seeps into the ground depends on the type of soil you have. Water is quickly absorbed in sandy soils but seeps slowly into heavier loams and clays. The soil type also determines the spread of the water flowing through the soil.

If water is applied in a narrow band (through trickle irrigation) on sandy soils, the water will seep in quicker and deeper than on a heavier soil. On loams and clay, the water spreads out more and requires larger amounts to reach the same depth. Excess

water on a sandy soil could leach below the area where most of the roots are found. Leaching water is also likely to take some soil nutrients with it, especially nitrogen. This requires you to add more fertiliser than you may otherwise need.

Splashing your plants with soil when watering can cause the spread of soil borne diseases such as Target Spot (*Alternaria solani*) and Bacterial Speck (*Pseudomonas syringae*).

Using hoses or sprinklers

Most people water their gardens with sprinklers. In drought areas or during water restrictions often hand held hoses are the only option. Unfortunately most of us do not have the patience to stand in the garden for the length of time needed to water properly.

To illustrate this, try to guess how much water you would need to properly irrigate tomatoes planted in a bed 6 x 1 metre (20 feet long and three feet wide).

Tomatoes need a minimum of 2.5cm (one inch) of water per week, preferably 4cms (1.5 inches) in the heat of the summer. 2.5cm (one inch) of water on 6 square metres (60 square feet) would require about 110 litres (30 gallons). That's the minimum amount needed in one week and you could easily double this amount in the summer.

So lets say you need to apply 200 litres (50 gallons) and your hose at full blast provides 8 litres (2 gallons) a minute. You would need to stand there for 25 minutes to provide enough water for the plants. Unfortunately, even if you have the patience to stand there that long, most of the water will probably runoff anyway. The result, uneven watering that barely gets into the soil. The lesson here is don't water by hand and at the very least, buy a sprinkler.

Although sprinklers are superior to hand watering, there are still disadvantages. Overhead watering results in wet leaves which can lead to a greater level of disease, both bacterial and fungal. When the foliage is wet, stay out of the tomatoes since that is a perfect time to spread disease.

To minimize the length of time the leaves remain wet, we recommend that you water in the morning so that the leaves will dry out during the day. Watering the entire garden also encourages weeds to germinate between the rows. Mulch can take care of the weeds between the rows, however not when you use plastic mulch.

With overhead irrigation on plastic mulch, little water gets into the bed but instead runs off between the rows, wasting water.

Trickle and Drip Irrigation

The most efficient way to water is the method used by many professional growers, using a trickle or drip irrigation system.

Water is slowly applied through a hose or tube which decreases the amount of water needed by 50% or more. Little water is lost to evaporation. It is uniformly applied right at the roots. Leaves remain dry, disease may be reduced, and you can water at any time, day or night, whatever fits your schedule. You

can even water while working in the garden! Try that with a sprinkler!

Trickle irrigation is more costly to set up and will take some additional time. But the cost and time is a small price to pay for a system so easy to operate that it requires no more than turning a tap to water the entire garden.

Many of the components can be used year after year so the cost beyond the first year is minimal. You can even add fertiliser through a trickle irrigation system, spoon feeding your plants and preventing leaching and over application of nutrients.

Finally, you don't need any plumbing skills. Anyone can set up one of these systems with just a little guidance.

There are basically two types of trickle irrigation you can use.

The easiest to use is the soaker hose which has tiny pores along its entire length. Water leaks out of the hose slowly and evenly at about 2 litres (1/2 gallon) of water per minute per 30 metres (100 feet) of hose. Depending on your soil type, the water will spread half a metre (2 to 3 feet) across the top of the bed.

The second type of trickle irrigation is the kind that professional growers use. These are plastic tubes (trickle tapes) with holes spaced evenly along its length. The holes or emitters are spaced at either 20, 30, 45 or 60cm (8, 12, 18, or 24 inches). In general the 30cm (12 inch) spacing would be recommended for sandy soils and the 45cm (18 inch) spacing for loams and clay soils. Don't

Most of us don't have the time or patience to hand water, as it needs to be done slowly to reduce leaching

Trickle or drip irrigation delivers a steady supply of water to the roots of the plant

Photo: Courtesy US Dept Agriculture: Agricultural Research Service worry about the spacing of your tomatoes, the trickle tape, like the soaker hose, will provide a continuous zone of moisture.

In general the trickle tape is more versatile than the soaker hose. Although both are effective in slowly providing water, soaker hoses are not very effective when stretched more than 60 metres (200 feet) for a single bed. Also, if the water you are using is very hard or your source of water is from a pond or rainwater, you will be better off with the trickle tape. Water containing impurities will more likely clog the soaker hose even after filtering.

You can find irrigation kits at many garden centres and speciality irrigation stores. There's all sorts of add-ons you can purchase to maximise the efficiency of your irrigation system, including filters to keep the emitters unclogged and a timer to automate the watering process.

Trickle irrigation operates on the principle of applying water using low pressure. The easiest way to lower your tap pressure is by putting a pressure regulator on the hose. Regulators are designed to keep the pressure constant at 30 PSI, ensuring uniform watering.

In addition, you can purchase a fertiliser injector that will automatically mix fertiliser with the irrigation water at the proper amounts. All of these parts can be hooked up right to the tap.

From there, connect a standard garden hose and bring that to the garden. You now have a hose that is sitting at the garden ready to be hooked up to the trickle system.

Filter washer traps water supply sediment to prevent clogging of drippers

Adding a timer to your irrigation system is a good way to ensure your plants receive a regular and even supply of water

In the garden, lay one irrigation line (either trickle tape or soaker hose) for each row of tomatoes, a few centimetres or inches to the side of the plant.

The lines should run parallel to each other and all end at one side of the garden. The lines could be buried a couple of inches deep and covered with soil or put on the top of the bed and covered with plastic or organic (straw, grass clippings, paper, etc.) mulch.

Put an end cap at one end of the trickle tape or soaker hose. On the other end, you need to connect the irrigation lines to plastic tubing. Do this using T connectors. You will need one T for each irrigation line you place in the garden.

Connect the blank tubing to the garden hose using a hose connector. Once that connection is made, the system is ready to go.

The next question to ask yourself is how often should you run your irrigation system. The answer depends on a number of factors. Let's use an example to illustrate our point.

Lets say you have planted four rows of tomatoes, each row is 7.5 metres (25 feet long). That means that each row takes up about 4 square metres (50 square feet) (with a ½ metre or 2 foot bed width). It makes no difference how far apart you have spaced your plants, we only need to know how long the tomato row is.

You will need about 100 litres (25 gallons) per bed to provide 2.5cm (one inch) of water on 7.5 square metres (50 square feet). Now let's take all those numbers and figure out how long to run our system.

The soaker hose will deliver 110 litres (30 gallons) of water per hour per 30 metres (100 feet) of hose. That means on our 7.5 metre (25 foot) long tomato bed we will be applying 28 litres (7.5 gallons) of water per hour. We will need to run the system for a little more than three hours each week to give us the minimal amount of water for our plants. For best results, water three times per week at two hours each time so the ground stays relatively moist. Of course if it rains, you can cut back on the watering.

If you are using trickle tape, you need to know the emitter spacing (spacing between holes in the tape) and how much water will come out of each hole over time. If you purchase tape with emitters spaced every 45 cm (18 inches) and each emitter will have about 4 litres (one gallon) seep out over one hour. A 7.5 metre (25 foot) row of tomatoes would have about 16 emitters. If each emitter puts out 4 litres (1 gallon) per hour, that means you would need to run the system for about 90 minutes to supply the minimum amount of water. We recommend running the system about 1 hour every other day, assuming you have no rain.

From time to time, trickle pipes will need cleaning, particularly if the water comes from a bore hole or dam where water may have a high calcium or some algal content. You can buy commercial irrigation cleaning products from specialist irrigation shops or larger hardware stores.

Watering pots

Because the volumes of soil are relatively small, containers can dry out very quickly, especially on a concrete patio in full sun. Daily or even twice daily watering may be necessary.

Apply water until it runs out the drainage holes. The soil should never be soggy or have water standing on top of it. When the weather is cool, container plants may be subject to root rots if maintained too wet.

Clay pots and other porous containers facilitate evaporation from the sides of the pots, so watering must be done more often. Small pots also tend to dry out more quickly than larger ones.

If the soil appears to be drying excessively fast (plants wilting every day is one sign), group the containers together so the foliage creates a canopy to help shade the soil and keep it cooler.

Mulching and windbreaks can help reduce water requirements for containers. If you are away a lot, consider an automatic drip emitter irrigation system.

Water Quality

Tomatoes are moderately tolerant of saline water, especially if applied by drip or trickle irrigation. Tomatoes will all tolerate up to 4000 ppm of dissolved salts providing there is good drainage. Where it is applied overhead, either by irrigation or by hose, and comes into contact with the leaves, tomato plants are more sensitive to saline water because of the level of salt on the foliage. Some reduction in yield may occur and blossom-end rot may be more of a problem on the fruit.

A drip irrigation system can be set up for pots

There are a variety of self-watering pots available

9. Nutrition

Nutrient application needs to be balanced to achieve early vigorous vegetative growth followed by heavy flowering and fruit set.

Before we get into the detail of nutrition, it is worthwhile recapping on soil types and pH, as these have a bearing on how much nutrition your plants will take up from the soil.

Understanding your soil

Tomatoes will grow in a wide variety of soil types and across a wide range of pHs although they prefer a pH between 5.5 – 6.8.

In order to understand your soil type it is essential that you have an understanding of what pH is and how it may affect the nutrition of your tomatoes.

The term pH defines whether your soil, is acid or alkaline. The pH scale runs from 0 – 14 with 7 being neutral. Numbers below 7 indicate acidity and above 7 alkaline. Most soils have a pH in the range 4.5 to 8.5. Tomatoes enjoy a slightly acid soil usually with a pH around 6.5.

The availability (uptake of nutrients from the soil by the plant) of nutrients is affected by soil pH. This is amply demonstrated by the chart below. This shows that

most nutrients have greater availability at pHs around 5.5 – 6.

pHs can be adjusted: lime will make the soil more alkaline and whilst making the soil more acid is more difficult, usually sulfate-based fertilisers (e.g. sulphate of ammonia) and acidic organic material will help.

Testing soil pH can be done simply by mixing soil and water and testing it using a pH meter, testing kit or litmus paper.

Soil type

Soil type will determine how much nutrient your soil can hold. Sandy soil types hold very little nutrient, whilst clays hold greater amounts. Soil type will therefore determine the amount of fertiliser you will require for your tomatoes.

Sandy soil types will require a higher rate of fertiliser as well as more frequent applications because fertilisers get leached out in sandy soils. In other words, when water is applied, because sandy soils are so porous, the water runs straight through taking with it the nutrients that are required by the plant.

Fertilising for the Home Gardener

Starter Fertiliser

All plants enjoy substantial amounts of organic matter – manure or compost in the soil. Organic matter holds nutrients in the soil so that they are not lost through leaching. It increases the amount of water your soil can hold as well as microbial activity in the soil, encouraging earthworms and creating a wonderful healthy

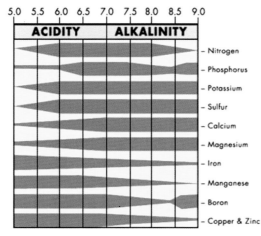

Fig 1: The effect of soil pH on plant nutrient availability

soil system that produces nice sweet tomatoes.

Compost in the soil takes time to break down and release its nutrients– often up to 2 – 3 months. This means that if you want to use compost alone, it should be dug into the soil at least a month before you wish to plant your tomatoes.

It often helps to add a bit of fertiliser (even if you have used compost) at 5cm (2 inches) below and 5cm (2 inches) to the side of where you plant your seedling. If you put fertiliser directly in contact with the roots you will burn them and your tomato seedling may die or its growth be retarded.

Understanding Fertiliser Units

All fertilisers are generally described by their analysis. This usually consists of 3 figures that respectively label the percentage of Nitrogen (N), Phosphorus (P) and Potassium (K) in a product.

The sequence of N, P and K never changes. However in the USA these units are designated as N - P_2O_5 – K_2O whilst in other countries (such as Australia) the units are N-P-K.

P_2O_5 means phosphate in the oxide form, as opposed to phosphorus (used in Australia) and K_2O is the oxide form of potassium whilst in Australia only K or potassium is used.

What to put on and how much

Organic matter – a minimum of 3kg/m^2 should be applied one month before planting.

Calcium - if available, at the same time also add 200 – 300g/m^2 (6 – 8oz/yd^2) of lime, dolomite or gypsum and dig in

along with the compost. This will provide your tomatoes with a source of calcium which will enhance their quality and shelf life.

Nitrogen – broadcast and incorporate 8g/m^2 or 1 ½ tsp/m^2 (0.2oz/yd^2) of nitrogen as a starter. Further nitrogen will be applied as top dressings.

Do not over-fertilise, especially with nitrogen, as your plants may produce lots of leaf but no flowers. Over-fertilising can also burn your plant. If nitrate fertiliser is available, this will give you a form of nitrogen that your plant can easily access.

Wherever you purchase your fertiliser, check the label or ask the technical salesperson for a rate of application for tomatoes. This will vary depending on the analysis of the fertiliser and should always be checked prior to application.

Also remember that only one third of the total plant requirement should be applied at planting. The balance will need to be applied in separate lots of one third (see top dressings).

Phosphorus - is essential for root development. At least 15 - 20g/m^2 or 3 – 4 teaspoons/ m^2 (0.4 – 0.6oz/yd^2) of phosphate (P_2O_5) or 6 - 9g/m^2 (1 – 2 teaspoons) of phosphorus (P) will be required. All the phosphate or phosphorus that the plant requires should be incorporated into the soil before planting. This is for several reasons – firstly it is required for root development, and also as it breaks down slowly, it is best to put it all in at the beginning.

Potassium - should be applied at 25g/m^2 K_2O (5 teaspoons) or 20g/m^2 K (4 teaspoons)

Before transplanting, dig in compost supplemented with a premixed fertiliser to enrich your soil

as a starter and dug in. This makes up 1/3 of the plant's requirements. Refer to the top dressing section for further recommendations.

Alternatively use a complete fertiliser such as
    5-10-10
    5-20-20 or
    8-16-16
and work this into the bed about two weeks before planting. Ask the store's technical salesperson for rates of application as this will vary according to the analysis of the fertiliser.

Top Dressing

Splitting the application of nitrogen and potassium into at least three applications over the life of the crop is more effective as it gives the plants access to nutrition when they most need it. After applying the basal amounts of nitrogen and potassium at planting, the next third should be applied at first flower and the final third about three weeks later.

The amounts to be applied at these stages are:

N – 8g/ m2 or 1.5 teaspoons/ m2 (0.2oz/ft2) at each application

K – 25g/m² K_2O (5 teaspoons) or 20g/ m² K (4 teaspoons) at each application

Both the nitrogen and potassium should be sprinkled in the area around the plant making sure that none touches the stem. Ensure the fertiliser is evenly spread so that there are no 'dollops' or lumps that can dissolve and burn the plant's roots.

Also make sure that none of the plant roots are exposed in any way before doing any

top dressing with granular fertilisers.

It is not always necessary to use granular fertilisers for top dressings. Liquid fertilisers are very effective. Be sure to follow the label rates as too strong a dose can burn your plant. Also make sure that liquid fertilisers are applied in the cool of the day (late afternoon is best).

Trace Elements

For the most part, the above nutrition program will be sufficient for most home gardeners. Occasionally your tomatoes will show that they are actually short of a trace element (please consult the key to show which element may be limiting) and sometimes there may be a shortage of several trace elements.

There are many granular and liquid trace element products on the market. Unless you know which trace element is deficient, it's best to purchase a multi-trace element fertiliser. The liquid products can be applied quite safely with a hand sprayer However, read the warnings on the container and dress appropriately whenever spraying your plants.

Application of Liquid Fertilisers

Liquid fertilisers have detailed instructions for application on the bottle label. Read these carefully and apply appropriately. There will usually be a dilution. For example, a dilution of 1:100 will mean apply 1 part of product to 100 parts of water. On other occasions, the dilutions may already have been done and you only need to measure and spray the liquid onto your plants.

Granular fertilisers should be evenly sprinkled around the plant, without touching the stem.

Diluted liquid fertilisers can be applied using a watering can, hand sprayer, venturi or fed through an irrigation system

Nitrogen deficiency

Photo: with permission of Epstein, E. and Bloom, A.J. (2005) Mineral Nutrition of Plants: Principles and Perspectives.

The four on the right show poor colouring. There is no gradual transition between red & green

www.agnet.org/library/article/pt2003021.html

Phosphorus deficiency

Photo: with permission of Epstein, E. and Bloom, A.J. (2005) Mineral Nutrition of Plants: Principles and Perspectives.

Potassium deficiency

Photo: with permission of Epstein, E. and Bloom, A.J. (2005) Mineral Nutrition of Plants: Principles and Perspectives.

Application of Granular Fertilisers

More is not better when it comes to fertilisers because they can easily burn your plants. Be careful to adhere to the recommended rates. Always double check the application rate with your store's technical salesperson and remember that different soil types may require different quantities of fertiliser. If in doubt, using a smaller quantity more frequently is better than lots in one go. Make sure you sprinkle evenly and that there are no big clumps which could burn your plants roots.

Nutrition Problems

Nitrogen Deficiencies

Nitrogen is one of the basic elements that a plant cannot do without. It is the building block for proteins and is also used in chlorophyll – the green matter in plants where photosynthesis occurs.

A shortage of nitrogen shows up as a yellowing of lower leaves which progresses upwards whilst lower leaves die – if not treated. Plants grow slowly, new leaves are small, thin and may have purple veins. Stems are hard and thick and eventually brown off and dry off. Flower buds turn yellow and drop, and the fruit is reduced in size and number and may be pale green (instead of dark green) before ripening.

Nitrogen Excess

Excess of application is more common than deficiency. Your plants will rapidly grow into quite bushy plants with many bright, light green leaves. You won't get many flowers and consequently little fruit. Those fruit that are set are poor

quality and soft, and very prone to diseases.

Phosphorus deficiencies

Phosphorus is another basic element required by plants in large quantities. It is used at all growth stages, but particularly early in the plant's life. It is necessary for cell division, growth and root and shoot development.

Deficiencies usually occur early in the growing season when the soil is still cool. Phosphorus is abundant in many soils but may be unavailable to the plant when the soil is too cold, so it's best not to plant tomatoes too early in the season. Once soil temperatures rise, the problem usually corrects itself.

Symptoms show up as plants with very dark green leaves which may have an inter-veinal purple colouration on the backs of leaves. Stems are thin, hard and fibrous and the fruit is pale in colour. Plants are stunted and the fruit set is delayed and usually the yield will be poor. Symptoms usually show up in the old leaves first.

Potassium Deficiencies

Potassium is an element that is required in large amounts when the plants are fruiting. It is essential for colour, disease resistance, root and crop maturity and vital for regulating the plant's water use.

A lack of potassium is indicated by plants that have dark green older leaves which become curled and crinkled. The leaves will start to die and the tissue between the veins breaks down. The fruit ripens unevenly and the fruit tend to be blotchy in colour with little fleshy tissue in them. The stems and sepals on the fruit yellow and become necrotic and the fruit drops off as soon as it is mature.

Calcium deficiency

Photo: with permission of Epstein, E. and Bloom, A.J. (2005) Mineral Nutrition of Plants: Principles and Perspectives.

Calcium deficiency also causes blossom end rot

Photo: Courtesy Sarah Browning, University of Nebraska- Lincoln Extension

Magnesium deficiency

Photo: with permission of Epstein, E. and Bloom, A.J. (2005) Mineral Nutrition of Plants: Principles and Perspectives.

Zinc deficiency

Photo: with permission of Epstein, E. and Bloom, A.J. (2005) Mineral Nutrition of Plants: Principles and Perspectives.

Calcium

Calcium is one of the most critical elements in tomatoes. It is very important for fruit quality, shelf life and disease resistance. It also helps the plant absorb other nutrients. However, it is one of the most difficult elements for plants to take up.

A lack of calcium causes thick, woody stems, slow growth, yellow upper leaves and weak, flabby plants. Young leaves, which develop symptoms first, exhibit tip burn which develops into a necrosis of the leaf margins. The plant feeder roots turn brown and die. Fruit are small, soft and have poor shelf life. Blossom end rot of the fruit is one of the main symptoms.

Blossom end rot: begins as light tan, water-soaked scars on the blossom end of the fruit. These scars enlarge and turn black and leathery. The cause is thought to be a combination of cold temperatures or excessive heat during blossom set, and fluctuations in water supply. When these two factors occur simultaneously, calcium often becomes unavailable to the plant. Hence, a calcium deficiency occurs during fruit formation. To manage the problem, fertilise and water properly. Avoid setting out transplants too early in the season. Use mulch to help reduce fluctuations in moisture levels.

Magnesium

Magnesium is the only element required by the plant that is actually involved in the structure of chlorophyll, the green pigment in plants that is involved in photosynthesis.

Deficiencies often occur at the vegetative growth stage, when magnesium is most required by the plant. It shows up on older leaves first as inter-veinal yellowing. When a shortage shows up later in the plant's life, it is not so important. However it does result in soft, pale coloured fruit.

Zinc

Worldwide zinc is one of the elements that is in short supply in many soils. It is important for growth as it is involved in the functioning of one of the essential growth hormones in the plant. It is also necessary for the photosynthesis process and is involved in pollen tube formation.

Deficiencies of zinc are more likely to show up when weather is cool or wet,. Symptoms show in young leaves first. New leaves are small, sometimes long and narrow with inter-veinal chlorosis. The chlorosis can be almost white resulting in dead spots. Leaf margins roll upwards; pollination and fruit set is low and the skin has a poor texture. Internodes become shorter which results in a whorl-type growth pattern of leaves at the end of stems or branches.

Manganese

Manganese is important in the vegetative growth stage of plants, however it is not frequently a problem on tomatoes.

If deficiency symptoms develop, they'll show up in new leaves first. The leaves will be pale green with mottled inter-veinal chlorosis which progresses to dead patches ringed in yellow

Manganese deficiency

Photo: with permission of Epstein, E. and Bloom, A.J. (2005) Mineral Nutrition of Plants: Principles and Perspectives.

Iron deficiency

Photo: with permission of Epstein, E. and Bloom, A.J. (2005) Mineral Nutrition of Plants: Principles and Perspectives.

Copper deficiency

Photo: with permission of Epstein, E. and Bloom, A.J. (2005) Mineral Nutrition of Plants: Principles and Perspectives.

Boron deficiency

Photo: with permission of Epstein, E. and Bloom, A.J. (2005) Mineral Nutrition of Plants: Principles and Perspectives.

Molybdenum deficiency

Photo: with permission of Epstein, E. and Bloom, A.J. (2005) Mineral Nutrition of Plants: Principles and Perspectives.

and premature leaf drop. There will be few flowers and fruit and growth is very slow.

Iron

Lack of iron is seldom seen on tomato plants although it can be a problem on soils high in calcium or with a high pH. Iron is used in the respiration processes and is involved in energy production in the plant. It is also essential for chlorophyll formation although it is not a constituent of chlorophyll.

Symptoms of a lack of iron show as chlorosis on new leaves with the youngest leaves being the first affected. New leaves have spotted white areas and the tips and margins of leaves lose their green colour last. Affected leaves curl upwards and may drop. New shoots may die if severely deficient. Fruit may not mature completely and drop off.

Copper

Rarely a problem in tomatoes, when it does occur it is noticeable because copper is required for the lignin (strengthening tissue) in plants. Without it plants have stunted root and shoot growth, blue-green curled, flabby leaves with few or no flowers and a soft stem. Symptoms show in new growth first.

Boron

Boron is required throughout the life of a tomato plant. The plant cannot take up calcium unless it has boron. When it is in short supply the plant shows symptoms on new growth first. Blackened areas develop at the tip of the stem, which is stunted. The plants look abnormally bushy and the terminal shoots curl,

turn yellow and die. Leaves may be discoloured, crinkled, deformed, brittle and small. Fruit of severely affected plants may be misshapen, split, corky and darken and die in patchy patterns.

Molybdenum

Molybdenum is an important element in tomato plants even though it is used in the minutest amounts. It is used to convert nitrates to ammonium which is used in the synthesis of amino acids and thence proteins in plants. Often what appears as a nitrogen deficiency is actually a shortage of molybdenum. Deficiency symptoms are very similar to those for nitrogen – with the exception that application of nitrogen makes the symptoms worse, especially death of the leaf tips.

Shortage symptoms show as a cupping or curling of leaf margins, yellowing between veins and small size of new leaves. Necrosis (death) of leaf margins and tips can also occur.

10. Pests and Diseases

Damping Off affects seedlings.
Photo: Courtesy T.A. Zitter,
Cornell University, Ithaca, NY

Fusarium Wilt
Photo: Courtesy Randy Gardner,
North Carolina State University

Fusarium Crown Rot
Photo: Courtesy University of Florida,
Institute of Food and Agricultural Sciences

Common Tomato Diseases

Tomatoes can be seriously affected by pests and diseases, particularly in warm wet climates. Because a home garden will probably only have five to 10 tomato plants, there may be no opportunity to replant (because of weather restrictions) if some plants are lost to pests and diseases. It is therefore very important to monitor established plants regularly and act quickly if there are symptoms of pests or diseases.

Diseases may be caused by fungi, bacteria and viruses.

Damping Off

Symptoms

The term 'damping off' refers to the death of young seedlings, either after emergence or after transplanting. The stem of the seedling turns brown or black at soil level and withers causing death of the plant. This is commonly caused by any one of three diseases – *Pythium, Rhizoctonia* or *Phytophthora*.

Damping off is a problem in cold, wet soils or in cool, damp weather. It can also be caused by crowding of seedlings, over watering, lack of air circulation or contaminated pots, soil or water.

Control

Whilst fungicides are available for these diseases, it is preferable not to use them in home gardens. Instead, ensure the soil is well drained, the plants adequately ventilated and the weather relatively warm before planting out.

Use high quality seed. Make sure all organic matter in the soil is decomposed and no

mulch is actually touching the seedlings. An old remedy is to dip seedlings in chamomile tea before planting and pour the rest around the seedling after transplanting.

Diseases Causing Wilts

Wilts can be caused by both fungi and bacteria. They cause the plants to wilt or go limp as if short of water and this may be accompanied by shortages of nutrients causing yellowing of leaves.

The plant is in fact short of water and nutrients because the vascular system of the plant (water conducting system) is blocked as a result of infection. Cutting open the stem of the plant lengthwise will reveal a brown discoloration of the vascular system.

There are several types of wilt diseases:

Fusarium

- Fusarium (*Fusarium oxysporum f.sp. lycopersici*)
- Fusarium Wilt
- Fusarium Crown Rot

Symptoms

Symptoms begin as yellowing of older leaves which later turn downward and droop, and eventually the whole plant wilts. In mild cases the plant may just grow slowly or be pale and stunted.

With Fusarium Crown Rot, the leaves often turn brown or black and eventually wilt and the stem may rot at the base or crack. Fusarium oxysporum, the cause of both Fusarium Wilt and Crown Rot, is a common tomato fungus that lives in the plant's vascular system.

53

To see if either of these diseases is present:

- Check watering practices. Both over- and under-watering can mimic disease symptoms.

- Check the roots. Discoloured roots indicate root rot.

- Cut the lower or main stem and look inside at the vascular tissue. Fusarium Wilt causes a reddish-brown discoloration within the vascular tissue. Fusarium Crown Rot causes a rot or canker at the base of the stem and possibly a Root Rot.

Unlike Verticillium, Fusarium is a disease of warmer weather and development of the disease usually occurs at high soil temperatures.

Control

Most commercially produced tomato seeds and seedlings are labelled VFN, meaning that they have been bred to be resistant to Fusarium Wilt (F) (as well as Verticillium and nematodes), so Fusarium Wilt is unlikely.

However if vascular discoloration is noted during the diagnostic process, pull and destroy affected plants.

Do not plant tomatoes, potatoes, capsicums or eggplant in the affected area for two or three years as there are no fungicides to control this disease.

This disease can last in the soil for a long time. If it is a known problem in your soil, try covering the soil with clear plastic sheeting for three weeks to kill off spores in the soil before planting out.

Verticillium (*Verticillium dahliae*)

Symptoms

In the US, Fusarium is most prevalent in the south and Verticillium in the north.

The first symptom of this disease is midday wilting and the plants then recover at night. The leaves turn yellow, showing a "v-shaped" lesion on the lowest leaves.

Verticillium Wilt is generally more prevalent in cooler weather and the symptoms are more pronounced when the plant has a heavy fruit load

As resistant cultivars are available (designated 'V'), when buying seed ask for those with the appropriate resistance for your location. Rotation of growing spot is also essential, being careful not to rotate with plants such as eggfruit or potatoes.

Bacterial wilt (*Ralstonia solanacearum*)

Bacterial wilt is a soil borne disease which infects the roots and stem of the plant causing a sudden wilt. The vascular system will once again be brown, and if the stem is cut and held in water a noticeable 'milk' will stream out of the stem. These are the bacteria.

Control

Crop rotation and sanitation are controls for this disease.

Verticillium Wilt

Photo: Queen's Printer for Ontario, 2005.
Reproduced with permission

Bacterial Wilt

Photo: Courtesy University of Georgia

Leaf Spots

Early Blight or Target Spot (*Alternaria solani*) is one of the most common tomato leaf diseases.

Symptoms

This disease produces brown to black, target-like spots (which appear to have concentric circles) on older leaves. If severe the fungus also attacks stems and fruit (sunken lesions). Affected leaves may turn yellow then drop, leaving the fruit exposed to sunburn.

Target spot occurs all year but is worst in winter when there is heavy dew, fog or moisture in warm weather.

Control

Use disease-free seed. Remove all diseased plant tissue on the ground and plant residues after harvest as this fungus survives on leaf debris and infected, decayed plant tissue.

Rotate crops with those other than tomatoes, potatoes and egg fruit. Sanitation is the best control. Do not plant tomatoes in the same place next year. Space plants farther apart to improve air circulation.

Avoid overhead irrigation. If the infestation is heavy, a registered fungicide may help protect new leaves from infection.

Septoria Leaf Spot (*Septoria* blight*)*

Symptoms

Older leaves have many, small, water soaked spots usually 1 – 2 mm diameter. Leaves may start to drop followed by progressive defoliation.

Control

Clean cultivation, destroy infected plants, stay out of tomatoes when the foliage is wet.

Late Blight (*Phytophthora infestans*)

Symptoms

Leaves infected with Late Blight develop water-soaked patches that turn brown. In humid weather there may be a white, downy growth on spots. Over time the spots expand rapidly and become brown to purplish-black as tissue dies. Plant may look "frosted".

Fruits can be affected at any stage. Large irregular, rough, brown-green lesions can be found on the fruit. The disease (which is devastating in potatoes) can also cause severe losses in tomatoes when conditions are favourable (cool, wet weather) resulting in severe defoliation.

Control

The only way to control this disease is with fungicides.

Anthracnose (*Colletotrichum spp*).

Symptoms

Small circular lesions about 0.5cm (¼ inch) in diameter on the leaves. Will also cause sunken spots on the fruit.

Control

Fungicides.

Powdery Mildew (various species)

Symptoms

White powdery patches on leaves. This disease often appears when the plant is stressed during hot weather.

Control

It is important not to water the leaves and improve air circulation around the leaves. There are various sulphur-

Early Blight

Photo: Courtesy Uni of Guelph

Late Blight

Photo: Courtesy AVRDC
The World Vegetable Centre

Septoria Leaf Spot

Photo: Courtesy Uni of Guelph

Anthracnose

Photo: Courtesy AVRDC
The World Vegetable Centre

Bacterial Speck showing effects on leaves and fruit

Photo: Queen's Printer for Ontario, 2005.
Reproduced with permission

Bacterial Spot

Photo: Queen's Printer for Ontario, 2005.
Reproduced with permission

Bacterial Canker on leaves and fruit

Photo: Queen's Printer for Ontario, 2005.
Reproduced with permission

Botrytis

Photo: Courtesy T.A. Zitter,
Cornell University, Ithaca, NY

based products available to help combat this disease. These should be used as preventatives in hot weather.

Bacterial Speck (*Pseudomonas syringae*)

Symptoms

Dark raised specks on the leaves and fruit, often prevalent during moist weather. Highly contagious and spreads in water.

Control

Do not move in the crop when wet. If irrigating, preferably use drip.

The disease can be carried via seed. Ensure clean seed and do not collect seed from an infected crop or plant.

Weekly spraying with a copper-based fungicide from flowering will help prevent this disease. Thorough coverage of leaves is essential.

As the disease can survive on weeds and plant debris, it is important to practice good hygiene and crop rotation.

Bacterial Spot (*Xanthomonas campestris pv vesicatoria*)

Symptoms

Similar to those for bacterial speck.

Control

Very difficult to control in the wet weather. Do not move about in the crop when the plants are wet.

Weekly spraying with a copper-based fungicide from flowering will help prevent this disease. Thorough coverage of leaves is essential.

Bacterial canker (*Corynebacterium michiganense*)

Generally occurs sporadically.

Symptoms

Lower leaves begin turning downward and dark to light brown streaks may develop on the leaf mid ribs, eventually extending down the petiole to form a canker on the stem. There may be vascular discoloration and a dry, hollow stem.

Symptoms on fruit are small, white, scabby, raised lesions, often described as "bird's eye."

Control

This disease is difficult to distinguish from other tomato diseases but if identified, destroy the plants. Do not compost plant material. Do not plant tomatoes, potatoes or eggplant in the same soil for two to three years. Use good quality seed.

Fruit Rots

Botrytis

Symptoms

A grey fluffy mould that grows on fruit, particularly if it is damaged. It is more prevalent during wet summers. It may also cause pale whitish ghost spots on fruit and leaves.

Symptoms

Cool, humid conditions are required for the development of the disease. Fungicides are available for control but otherwise allow good circulation around the tomato plants to reduce humidity and avoid irrigating in the afternoon and evening. Ensure any infected plant material is removed and destroyed.

Black Rot Mould (*Alternaria alternata*)

Symptoms

Large, black, sunken lesions in the tomato fruit. Like Early Blight, Black Rot mould lives on decaying plant tissue and requires wet conditions to infect the fruit.

Control

Remove dead and decaying plant material and ensure the fruit does not remain wet overnight. Fungicides can control the disease

Black Rot Mould

Photo: Courtesy University of Florida, Institute of Food and Agricultural Sciences

Root Rot

Root Rot can be caused by several fungi.

Symptoms

Often those associated with lack of roots i.e.: yellowing of all foliage and wilting.

Control

Unfortunately for home gardeners control of a potential root rotting fungus is almost impossible.

As poor soil drainage and over watering are the main cause, management of Root Rot requires soil improvement, proper watering, and rotation of tomatoes. Only plant tomatoes and related species in the same spot once every three years.

Root Rot

Photo: Courtesy University of Florida, Institute of Food and Agricultural Sciences

Virus diseases

Some of the viruses that affect tomatoes also affect alfalfa (lucerne), cucumber and other members of the Solanaceae family (to which tomatoes, potatoes, eggfruit and many weeds belong).

Once a virus has infected a tomato plant there is nothing that can be done to remove the virus from the plant. So prevention is the best way of ensuring the crop does not become infected.

Infection is usually as a result of insect pests such as aphids and thrips. Many common weeds and most other member of the Solanaceae family are hosts to these viruses.

Prevention of these viral diseases relies on keeping tomato plants away from other host plants (keeping the plants weed-free) and minimizing infestation by aphids and thrips by encouraging biological control of these pests.

Symptoms of viral diseases can be quite varied but may include stunting and deformations of leaves, stems and fruit as well as unusual mottling.

Tomato Spotted Wilt

Tomato Spotted Wilt/Impatiens Necrotic Spot Tospoviruses (TSWV or INSV) has traditionally been a problem in commercial tomato production. Recently, however, the disease has increasingly been found in home gardens.

Symptoms

Symptoms begin as dark brown to purple spots on leaves. The dark areas spread to stems, forming cankers. Stem streaking also may be noticed.

Wilting symptoms gradually develop as the disease spreads. However, the leaf tissue is stiff, not limp.

The most noticeable symptoms are yellow rings or spots on fruit. Fruit may be distorted.

TSWV and INSV move from plant to plant by western flower thrips. The only way to manage the disease is to remove and destroy affected plants.

Spotted Wilt Virus on leaves and fruit

Photos: Courtesy AVRDC
The World Vegetable Centre

57

www.bestjuicytomatoes.com

How to Grow Juicy Tasty Tomatoes

Curly Top Virus
Photo: Courtesy Colorado State University

Mosiac Virus
Photo: Courtesy AVRDC
The World Vegetable Centre

Root Knot Nematode
Photos: Courtesy AVRDC
The World Vegetable Centre

Thrips are extremely difficult to control.

Curly Top Virus

Curly top virus is transmitted by the beet leaf hopper and is a common problem in some areas of the US.

Symptoms

Infected plants turn yellow and stop growing. Upper leaflets roll and develop a purplish colour, especially along the veins. Leaves and stems become stiff; fruit ripens prematurely.

Control

Curly top virus is difficult to control because leaf hoppers in some areas of the US are migratory. Hot, dry springs with predominantly southwest winds usually indicate increased problems with this disease.

No chemical controls are effective. Use plant covers to protect tomato plants from the leaf hopper where this disease is a problem.

Mosaic Viruses

Symptoms

Yellow mottling and distortion of the leaves and fruit.

Control

This group of viruses is easily transmitted by hand, particularly by smokers who have been touching tobacco. Hygiene should be practised before handling tomato plants.

Nematodes

Root Knot Nematode

Symptoms

Slow stunted plant growth and possibly some yellowing. If a plant is pulled up, the roots will have bead-like structures all the way down. These are the

areas where the nematodes have invaded and are laying eggs (see separate section on nematodes).

Fungicides

Every country has its own list of government registered fungicides for different crops. Suppliers of these chemicals have to prove that they work, and usually that they will not cause undue damage to the grower and the environment.

The list of registered fungicides for home gardeners is quite small and in the case of tomatoes revolves around the use of two in particular. The "active" ingredient of one is mancozeb and the other is copper. Although every country and reseller usually has a different commercial or selling name for it's fungicides, in most cases the "active" chemical is the same.

Mancozeb is the active of products often used for leaf spotting diseases. Copper-based chemicals can also be used for leaf spotting diseases, but are best for bacterial diseases which mancozeb will not control. These chemicals should be applied prior to the plant getting the diseases as they will not control diseases that have already started on the plant.

Fungicides are best applied prior to rain, and then following rain before the appearance of disease. Fungicides will not control bacterial wilt-type diseases as well as some fungal wilts. However there are fungicides available for Phytophthora Root Rots.

Viral diseases are usually controlled by controlling the pest and practising good hygiene.

Common Pests

Cutworm

Damage is seen as plants (seedlings) that appear to have been cut off. This usually occurs at night and is caused by the larvae or caterpillars known as cutworms because of the manner in which they cut down young plants as they feed.

The adults are night-flying moths which may feed on nectar and do no damage. While they all feed on plants by chewing, they vary as to damage done and host plants preferred. Generally they destroy more of the plant than they eat.

Their numbers vary greatly from year to year and may destroy as much as 75% of plants when particularly prevalent. Damage often occurs during the first night after transplanting and may continue for up to three weeks.

Control

Remove weeds in the area to be planted well before transplanting.

In problematic areas a wax paper collar (about 7cm/3 inches) can be placed around the base of the stem (5cm / 2 inches above ground and 2cm / 1 inch below ground). Collars of old tin cans or old plastic soft drink bottles will also work or try two toothpicks as stakes on either side of seedlings. A well mulched soil will deter cutworms.

Aphids

Aphids cause leaf yellowing and leave a characteristic sticky excrement called honeydew which gives the plant a shiny and somewhat sticky appearance.

Aphids are the main transmitters of viral diseases, doing more damage in this way than physically. In fact in many instances, they will feed briefly (sucking sap) on the plant and then move on and so are not noticed. In this period of feeding they will transmit virus which they carry internally.

Control

Whilst broad spectrum insecticides can be used, these tend to kill the good as well as the bad insects. In the home garden, plants like basil may produce chemicals that repel aphids and can be planted close to tomatoes. Insecticidal soaps may also be used.

Thrips

Like aphids thrips are also involved in the transmission of some viral diseases. Damage caused by thrips generally tends to be minimal although their feeding may cause distortions to leaves and fruit. For the home gardener, these fruit will still be usable.

Thrips are very small (about 1mm long) and range from dark brown to pale yellow or white. Adults have two pairs of narrow wings. A number of different species are involved, two of which are the onion thrips (*Thrips tabaci*) and flower thrips (*Thrips obscuratus*).

Control

Biological control methods are the best to use in the home garden. This ranges from companion plants, (which deter thrips from landing) to plant oils (which stick to the insects) which decrease their movement and sticky traps which can be hung in amongst the plants.

Cutworm damage

Photo: Courtesy Purdue University

Aphids

Photo: Courtesy Ohio State University'

Thrip

Photo: Courtesy Office of International Research, Education and Development, Virginia Tech

Thrip damage

Photo: Courtesy Whitney Cranshaw, Colorado State University

Bollworm (Fruitworm)
Photo: Courtesy Clemson Entomology,
Clemson University

White Fly
Photo: Courtesy Cooperative Extension,
University of Arizona

Stink Bug
Photo: Courtesy Drees, Texas A & M University

Spider Mite damage
Photo: Courtesy University of Kentucky

Spider Mite
Photo: Courtesy Kansas State University

Tomato bollworm or fruitworm

This pest (*Helicoverpa spp*) is found on many different vegetable and commercial crops worldwide. It ranges in colour from green to yellow to pinkish red to chocolate brown depending on its growth stage. It has four pairs of pro-legs on its abdomen (whereas the looper only has two pairs). It tunnels into the fruit causing it to rot.

Control

There are many common predators (good bugs) in the home garden which will attack these bollworm such as parasitic wasps (parasiting the eggs or the caterpillar), shield bugs, spiders, ants, ladybirds, damsel bugs, lacewings and birds.

Pesticides are not recommended in the home garden for this pest. It can be picked off if it has not burrowed into the fruit, otherwise pick off the damaged fruit and destroy.

Whitefly

Adults are small (about 1mm long) and white and can sometimes be seen flying around the plants, whilst the immature flies (which are found on the underside of leaves) are oval, flat, yellow to white and scale-like pests.

All growth stages feed on the plant and secrete honeydew on which the sooty mould fungus can grow. Whitefly is more of a pest in greenhouse situations than in the open.

Control

Many parasitic insects (good bugs) are predators on whitefly. The range of predators is very similar to those for bollworm.

As whitefly are heavily attracted to the colour yellow; hanging yellow sticky traps in the midst of the crop is an effective control. Crop oils are also useful.

Chemical pesticides are not recommended for home use. Once the tomatoes have been harvested and the plants are finished they should be removed from the garden to eliminate over-wintering sites for whitefly.

Stink bugs

This insect is green or brown and shield-shaped and emits a pungent smell when disturbed. These bugs cause spots and internal damage to tomato fruit through their feeding.

Symptoms

Stink bug damage on green fruit appears as dark pinpricks surrounded by a light, discoloured area. As fruit ripens, these spots may remain green or turn yellow. The tissue underneath is white and spongy. Cavities may form under the damaged skin.

Control

As these insects over-winter in weeds around the tomato patch, keeping the area clean of weeds will assist in their control.

Spider mite

Symptoms

White-yellow speckling of the leaf surface resulting in decreased plant growth and finally death of the plant. These are usually only a problem in hot dry weather.

If the underside of the leaves are examined, small white or red mites can be seen moving around and possibly even some webbing may be seen. The spider mite goes through five stages (egg, larva, first nymph

60

and second nymph and adult).
All stages can usually be
observed.

Control

Frequently spray plants with
a mist of water as mites hate
moist conditions.

Fruit Fly

Symptoms

Small maggots in fruit.

Control

If tomatoes are picked regularly,
fruit fly maggots should not
be a problem. Do not leave
fallen fruit lying on the ground
and as a last resort, pick green
tomatoes and let them ripen
indoors or cover fruit with a
fruit fly-proof net.

Crickets

Symptoms

Black field crickets can destroy
seedlings by chewing on stems
at or close to ground level.

Control

Baits are used commercially,
but are not recommended for
the home garden. Look out for
cricket holes and fill with hot
water.

Slugs and Snails

These are less of a problem
for tomatoes than other fruit,
although they do enjoy nice
ripe fruit.

Control

Put a collar made from a plastic
soft drink bottle or from the
top of a tin can around the
stem or put pellets inside an
old ice cream container with a
little door cut out for the slugs
or snails to enter. This keeps the
pellets confined so that lizards,
other soil life, pets and children
do not have access to them.

Fruit Fly

Photo: Courtesy Invertebrate Pest Monitoring Unit,
Agriculture Western Australia

Cricket

Lorikeet caught in the act!

Photo: Annette's tomato garden

Birds

Symptoms

Peck marks in fruit.

Control

Picking fruit regularly will
eliminate any bird problem.
Otherwise use bird-proof nets.

Nematodes

Tomatoes are particularly
susceptible to nematodes. The
most prevalent of these is the
root knot nematode, so called
because of the 'knot-like'
structures it causes on the roots
of the plant.

Nematodes are microscopic
round worms – too small for
the eye to see. They generally
cause dysfunction of the roots,
reduced rooting volumes and
general malaise of the plant.

In many cases they can weaken
plants sufficiently that they
become prone to fungal and
other diseases, and in some
cases these nematodes actually
transmit viral diseases. Yield
reduction can be large, but
varies with cultivar and more
particularly, with soil type.
Nematodes are generally a
much bigger problem in sandy
soils than other soil types.

Symptoms

These can involve both aerial
and root plant parts. The
plant appears unthrifty, can be
stunted (depending on degree
of infection), wilts prematurely
and only recovers slowly once
watered. Other symptoms
resemble those of nutrient
deficiencies as a result of the
loss of root mass. Sometimes,
fruit can colour up prematurely
as a result of increased ethylene
production (the hormone that
causes fruit ripening in plants).

How to Grow Juicy Tasty Tomatoes

The decline time period varies with nematode population and environmental conditions. For example, where there is a heavy infestation of root knot nematodes, seedlings may fail to develop or die soon after transplanting. Where the level of nematode infestation is not severe, evidence of infection may only occur once the population of nematodes has increased sufficiently for high levels of root damage to occur.

If nematode damage is suspected, it is best to pull up an unhealthy plant and examine the roots. Root knot nematode causes swollen areas or galls on the roots of infected plants. The size of the gall may vary from a few small 'knots' to extensive areas of tumorous, convoluted swellings which are the result of multiple infections.

Control

Nematodes are the main reason why crop rotation is so important. Growing the same crop or vegetable, particularly members of the solanaceous (nightshade) family, provides a continual source of nourishment to nematodes which will multiply exponentially in the soil.

Root knot nematodes are particularly difficult to eliminate from the soil. Growing alternate crops such as maize or sorghum or members of the grass family (and some legume crops) will discourage multiplication of nematodes. Members of the marigold family exude substances in the soil that nematodes dislike, so are a good rotation possibility.

In all cases, it is important that these rotation crops are planted at temperatures lower than 18ºC (65ºF) (which

is the nematode threshold temperature).

As many weeds are solanaceous and will provide a source of nutrition for nematodes, it is important to keep your tomatoes weed-free.

If growing hybrid tomatoes, select a nematode resistant variety (designated N), particularly if growing tomatoes in high risk areas such as sandy soils.

In all soil types regularly adding aged compost and manures will encourage the multiplication of beneficial microbes.

Safety

All registered pesticides, including fungicides for home gardeners will have been evaluated by local government authorities for human and animal safety. They should, therefore, be safe to use at the directed rates.

Most pesticides have a safety rating on them. Some countries have different coloured triangles on the front label with the warmer colours (oranges and reds) indicating the need for caution and extreme caution. In some countries, the warning is a written one on the front middle panel of the label e.g. **Warning: Handle with Caution** or **Keep Away from Children**. Always read the label thoroughly and wear the indicated safety gear.

Check the withholding period on the label (often shown under the directions for use). A withholding period indicates the allowable period between application of the chemical and eating it. A withholding period of seven days means that the crop/fruit etc, should not

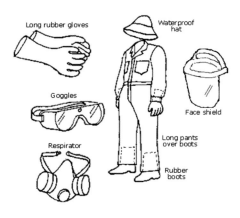

It is recommended that you wear protective clothing when spraying pesticides and herbicides

be eaten within seven days of applying the chemical.

It is essential to double check your calculations when using the label directed rate.

Physiological problems

Catfacing

Symptoms

Catface is a term that describes tomato fruit that is misshapen, with scars, growths and holes. The cause is thought to be cold weather during blossoming and perhaps high levels of nitrogen. It is most common in large-fruited beefsteak-type tomatoes.

Control

Avoid setting out transplants too early in the season.

Misshapen fruit

This can be due to poor pollination, possibly caused by very hot or very cold weather. Sometimes it can also be caused by a virus, but is usually accompanied by misshapen leaves and mottling.

Symptoms

Green/yellow shoulders develop on ripening fruit, possibly due to high temperatures. Chlorophyll in this area is slow to break down and results in a patch that remains green or turns yellow but not red. This problem may affect the entire shoulder or only a small, irregular patch.

Control

Shade the plant and take other precautions to reduce the fruit's exposure to the sun.

Sun scald

Sun scald is common on fruit exposed to too much sun. This problem often occurs in hot,

dry weather on plants where defoliation has taken place as a result of insect infestation, disease or where pruning has been too heavy.

Control

Shade the plant to allow recovery of foliage and reduce the fruit's exposure to the sun.

Blossom End Rot

Symptoms

A hard brown scab or dead area on the growing tip of the tomato.

This problem can be caused by high soluble salts, low soil calcium or inadequate soil moisture, or cool conditions slowing plant uptake of nutrients.

Control

Apply a calcium spray at weekly intervals for at least 3 weeks.

Blossom Drop

Can be caused by extreme weather such as a dry spell, drying soils or winds, heavy rains, sudden cold spells or things unrelated to weather such as heavy disease infections or overdoses of nitrogen.

Fruit Drop

Especially noticeable on early flowers, this problem occurs when night temperatures are lower than 12°C (55°F) or remain above 23°C (75°F)and when day temperatures are higher than 35°C (95°F).

Flower drop is also caused by plants that have dried out or are waterlogged, insufficient light, too much nitrogen, spraying at incorrect rate and thrips. Hot dry winds may intensify the problem.

Catfacing

Photo: Courtesy Carrie Lapaire Harmon
University of Florida

Sun scald

Photo: Courtesy Missouri Botanical
Garden PlantFinder

Blossom End Rot

Photo: Courtesy John Howell,
University of Massachusetts

Fruit Crack

Symptoms

Surface cracks in fruits near the stem end which can radiate around the stem and encircle the shoulders of the tomato. The depth of the cracks varies.

This is usually caused by rapid growth during periods of high temperature and good moisture or over-watering, or uneven wetting and drying periods. Tomatoes exposed directly to the sun are more prone to cracking. Fruit cracking varies by variety.

Control

Implement a regular watering program that minimises fluctuations in soil moisture. Mulch will help prevent periods of uneven growth and retain the moisture in the root zone for longer. Choose varieties which are less susceptible to cracking.

Cracked fruit should be picked early to prevent rots which may spread to other tomatoes.

Leaf Roll

Symptoms

This is most common on early-season varieties and plants that have been pruned. Leaf roll starts on the lower leaves and progresses up the plant. Some loss of leaf may occur, especially on staked plants.

This is not a disease and is most common on plants that are trained and pruned. Fruiting is not affected by this condition.

Control

Do not prune too heavily or cultivate too close to the plant.

Poor Fruit Set

This may be caused by too much nitrogen, particularly if foliage is dense and dark green.

Use mulch and compost and be careful about addition of further manufactured fertilisers.

Some varieties do not set well under certain weather conditions e.g.: cold climate varieties may not set well in hot weather. Plants drying out between watering cycles or leaf wilt in hot weather may also cause this.

Poor pollination (sometimes caused by lack of certain micronutrients) also affects fruit set. Hand pollination may be necessary to ensure a decent crop.

Chemical Toxicities

2.4-D or herbicide injury

This is unlikely in a home garden unless there is drift from a nearby farm or someone using a herbicide on their lawn. It can drift from as far away as one kilometre (half a mile).

Sprayers that have been used for herbicide and then used for disease and insect control on tomatoes may also be a source of contamination.

Symptoms

Twisted stems, fruit abnormalities, distorted leaves, dropping of flowers.

Control

Ensure herbicide sprayers are kept separate from applicators for insecticides and fungicides.

Walnut Toxicity

Symptoms

Plants growing near black walnut trees may wilt and die.

Control

Avoid growing tomatoes within 20 metres (50 feet) of walnut trees or where there is a possibility the roots of tomatoes will come into contact with the roots of the tree.

Fruit Cracking
Photo: Courtesy University of Massachusetts

Leaf Roll
Photo: Courtesy University of Kansas

11. Picking & Storage

Many commercially marketed tomatoes are picked green and artificially ripened with ethylene gas, leaving them odourless. Vine-ripened tomatoes exude that wonderful tomato fragrance.

When to Pick

Tomatoes should be picked before they are fully coloured, when they are still quite firm. This means that the plant can divert it resources to the next fruit. The picked tomatoes can then be ripened at room temperature. After they have reached full colour, store them in the refrigerator, or better still eat them whilst they are at their best.

Frost will destroy tomatoes, so if there is a threat of frost, harvest them and ripen indoors.

On the day before a killing freeze is expected, harvest all green mature fruit that is desired for later use in the fall. Wrap the tomatoes individually in paper and store at 15-18°C (60 to 65°F. They continue to ripen slowly over the next several weeks. Whole plants may be uprooted and hung in sheltered locations, where fruit continues to ripen.

1. Pick most kinds of tomatoes when their colour is even and glossy and the texture somewhere between soft and firm.

2. Watch the bottoms carefully; that's where tomatoes start to ripen. Some varieties, primarily large heirloom types, ripen before they reach full colour. Pick tomatoes when the skin still looks smooth and waxy, even if the top hasn't turned its mature colour (whether red, purple, pink or golden yellow).

3. Cut off the top of the plant, or remove all new flower clusters about a month before the first expected frost. That way, you'll direct the plant's energy into ripening existing tomatoes rather than producing new ones that won't have time to mature.

4. Extend your harvest through light frosts by covering plants with tarpaulins or sheets, but when the first hard frost threatens, pick all remaining fruits.

5. Put unripe tomatoes in a cool dark place, arranging them in a single layer. Check frequently for holes, cracks or even tiny specks of rot and remove any damaged tomatoes immediately - they'll quickly transmit moisture and rot to healthy fruits.

How to Store

Store at room temperature for best flavour, refrigerating only those that are overripe. To ripen green tomatoes, place on a rack so that fruits are not touching and set in a warm location at 18-21°C (65-70°F) away from sunlight. To slow ripen green tomatoes, store in a cooler location at 10-13°C (50-55°F).

To speed the ripening process, put tomatoes in a paper bag with a banana or an apple. Ethylene gas given off by the fruit will hasten the ripening process.

Once you've picked tomatoes (whether fully ripe or not) keep them away from sunlight. They'll overheat and ripen unevenly.

12. Collecting Seed

Seed saving allows gardeners to experience the full cycle of life of the tomato, and even develop individual varieties to suit their own taste.

Scraping seeds from ripe tomatoes

Rinsing after fermentation

Spreading to dry out

Tomato seed should be collected from the ripe fruit and will require processing. Avoid collecting seed from very overripe or rotten fruit, because at this stage the fruit contains numerous fibres that entrap seed, making their extraction more difficult.

Collection can be done by scraping or squeezing out the pulp of the fruit into a cup, jar or bowl. Tomato seed is enclosed in a jelly-like sac, which requires a few days of fermentation to break down. The pulp is fermented in a container until the seed coating has broken down, and is best undertaken in an area away from the house as it can be a bit smelly. Fermentation also has the advantage of developing conditions that will kill some of the bacteria and fungi that are responsible for some diseases.

The time taken for fermentation varies, it can be as short as a day under hot conditions to four or five days in late autumn (fall). It is important that the brew is not allowed to dry out during fermentation, and if necessary a small volume of water can be added if it appears that it may dry out. Narrow containers with a low surface (such as a cup) are more convenient than broader containers such as a saucer.

If the seed is allowed to ferment too long, germination may take place, which can be identified by the appearance of tiny white roots extending from the seed.

Once the gel coat has broken down, water is added to the pulp and decanted a number of times until clean seed remains. Pieces of skin, flesh and unviable seed tend to be less dense than healthy seed, and can be separated through carefully manipulating the movement of the water in the container, as if you were panning for gold.

The seed is then dried by spreading it out on newspaper or paper towels and thoroughly drying in the sun. With this method the seed will stick to the paper, and can be cut into pieces when the time is right for sowing. Alternatively, seed can be dried on glass or porcelain, and then scraped off when dry. Larger quantities can be dried on trays lined with flywire. Whichever way seed is dried it must be done in a well-ventilated area, with the seed spread into a thin layer so that drying occurs rapidly. Warm humid conditions during drying could induce germination and should be avoided.

When drying seed of several varieties, it helps to label them so that mix-ups don't occur. Keep them well apart when drying so the wind doesn't blow seed from one container into another.

Seed should be stored under cool, dry conditions and protect from direct sunlight, ideally at 25% humidity and at temperatures of 15-20°C (60-68°F). Store them with silica gel in plastic or glass jars with tight-fitting screw-top lids.

Silica gel (which you can obtain from pharmacies) acts as a desiccant, absorbing moisture from the air and producing conditions of low humidity in the jar. Don't forget to label the jars with the storage date and use them within 4-6 years.

13. Growing organically

An organic gardener works in harmony with natural systems to minimize and continually replenish any resources the garden consumes.

Organic gardening has often been thought of as the preserve of eccentrics who refused to accept the self-evident truth that twentieth-century progress had transformed the ancient art of gardening. Why did they fiddle around with compost and garlic spray when modern fertilisers and insecticides were so much more efficient and easier to use?

Opinions have changed, and now most gardeners regard 'organic' as the most sensible way to garden, as the benefits of twentieth-century technology have come at a price. Chemical sprays and fertilisers have done much damage to the environment. We might not think that we can do much to change the world, but we can take sensible care of the one part of the environment we control: our own garden. And by doing so, we do make a difference, particularly when you add up all the home gardens in the country (and indeed the world), they represent a fair chunk of our environment.

Organic gardening is simply the application of common sense such as people have been practising for centuries. It involves digging manure into a planting bed, putting kitchen scraps onto a compost heap, using blood and bone on your tomatoes instead of sulphate of ammonia. There is so much satisfaction to be gained from spreading a rich compost you have made yourself rather than a bag of chemical fertiliser. You know that it will benefit not just the immediate growth of your plants, but the health of your soil for years

to come. You are working hand in hand with Nature, in harmony with her own rhythms.

In order to maintain a healthy organic garden it is worth spending a few minutes reviewing the cycle of life in the garden, so that you understand all the elements and their interdependence on each other. When it is in balance, it works perfectly. If one or more elements are out of balance, you will have problems.

In a richly forested area where a huge variety of plants grow abundantly without human intervention, you will notice that the forest floor will be covered by a thin layer of fallen leaves. The leaves are decaying and beneath them is the multitude of living that are digesting the organic matter and in their turn adding their own dead bodies to the soil. They range from worms and small insects down to microscopic bacteria and fungi, without whose presence the recycling process could never occur.

Humus

The result of the work of all these organisms is the wonderful substance called humus. It is a sort of black colloid and gives fertile soil its dark colour and sweet earthy smell. It sticks to the mineral particles that form the framework of the soil and fills in the gaps so that water and dissolved nutrients are held within the structure, to be made available to plants as they are needed.

Humus is gradually digested and yields its nutrients to plants, and unless it is constantly replaced it vanishes and the soil dies. The soil lives as long as the recycling process is not interfered with – but interference is precisely what happens in a garden. We don't return everything to the soil. We remove weeds to the compost heap, we eat our vegetables and send our own wastes elsewhere. We cut flowers and throw them in the garbage; we burn prunings and every time we do, we diminish the humus supply. We may even add poisonous chemicals that kill the micro-organisms. Clearly, we need to work to restore the balance.

Unless you replenish the organic matter from which the humus is continually being created, the soil will gradually die. Chemical fertilisers boost the growth of your plants for a little while, but they do not nourish the living creatures of the soil, or create humus.

Chemical fertilisers have other problems as well. To make them soluble, they contain all sorts of things the garden doesn't need. Sulphate of ammonia certainly yields nitrogen from the ammonia, but the sulphate part poisons worms, bacteria and fungi. Organic matter – material that was once alive – must be added continually to feed the humus.

Rich humus

Compost rich in worms

Make your own compost by recycling as much organic matter as possible from the garden itself. Fallen leaves, vegetable stalks, spent flowers – nothing should be wasted. Then bring in other matter from outside, your vegetable scraps, animal manure, blood and bone, lawn clippings, hair, newspaper, straw, etc. Refer to the chapter on composting for tips on making the ideal compost mix.

Adding Organic Matter

Tomatoes love lots of compost and manure. Ideally this should be dug into your site at least eight weeks before planting to give it time to break down and give good texture to your soil as well as generate beneficial microorganisms in your soil. Time is also required for the nutrients in the compost or manure to be released. Digging the compost or manure into the soil early will most likely cause a whole lot of weeds to grow which can then be weeded out before planting your tomatoes.

If you are preparing a new tomato bed, spread your compost and fork it in to mix it with the soil. Around established plants where you don't want to dig deep and disturb roots, spread it onto the surface as mulch. As it decomposes it will sift down into the soil and the worms will come up and take it down with them.

A more-or-less permanent mulch keeps the soil cool, smothers any weeds and conserves moisture. It takes time to build the humus, especially if it has been depleted by wasteful gardening and poisoned by indiscriminate use of insecticides, fungicides and artificial fertilisers. It takes time to get used to the idea of feeding the soil and not the plants.

The demand for compost is greatest late winter when planting beds are being made up and through spring when mulching gets underway for summer, but you can spread your compost as and when it suits you.

Is Compost a Good Fertiliser?

Just how good a fertiliser compost makes depends on how you measure it . The amounts of available nitrogen, potassium and phosphorus (the NPK figures) are rather low and variable when compared to artificial fertiliser. It doesn't force an instant spurt of growth; its benefit is the long-term

If your soil is naturally low in a particular element, you simply add the required elements to the heap, preferably in a form on which the micro-organisms can work. Anything rich in protein (blood and bone, urine, manure) will add nitrogen; bone meal supplies phosphorus; potash comes from wood ash or seaweed.

Manure

Manure remains the best of all fertilisers, with compost running a close second. Whilst the proportion of the three major nutrients that manure contains is rather low, and dollar for dollar artificial fertilisers do give more weight of nitrogen, phosphorus and potassium; manure rots down to make humus to benefit the soil and its micro-life.

When you buy manure, it is likely to be pretty fresh – and far too strong and 'hot' to use. You will need to leave it in a heap for six weeks or so; covered with a plastic sheet to keep the rain from leaching the nitrogen out. This also allows you to assess whether the manure contains a lot of weed seeds as they will germinate in this time. Those deep in the heap will probably be killed by the heat of fermentation and

any that come up on the surface can be put on the compost heap. Or if there is room in the bin you can simply dump the manure on the compost heap.

Types of Manure

Poultry: this is the hottest and the smelliest. It is so strong it needs to be used almost as sparingly as you might use an artificial fertiliser, and you might prefer to use it to enrich the compost heap rather than applying it directly to the garden. Pelleted and dehydrated poultry manure which is sold in bags can be put straight on the beds for a quick boost, but you should still be wary of allowing it come in contact with the plants themselves, as it can still burn.

Pigeon: Similar to poultry, but hard to find. The same goes for still more exotic fowl such as pheasants and peacocks. Most bird manure is rather alkaline when it is fresh, although it becomes less so as it mellows.

Horse: This ranks first among the dung of walking animals, which is all pretty much the same, and none is nearly as rich and sharp as that of birds. It is often raked out from stables rather than collected from paddocks and is a mixture of half-rotted straw or sawdust bedding wet with urine. It's the urine that burns, so it should be heaped and cooled down before you use it.

Mushroom Compost: Although sold as 'spent' mushroom compost, it is sometimes still quite hot – if it comes out of the bag warm and smelling strongly of ammonia, it is best heaped up under cover for a couple of weeks. It can be quite alkaline, so pH may need to be tested before adding to

Any type of manure should be heaped for six weeks or so before using

tomato beds. If your bed shows a pH of 7.5-8 or higher, you could try adding agricultural sulphur to reduce it.

Cow and Sheep manure are the next best, with Goat manure close behind. Again they are best heaped for a month.

Using Manure

Once it is nicely mellowed, manure can be dug into the soil or spread as a mulch. Like compost, manure acts slowly in releasing its nutrients, especially in winter when the nutrient-releasing bacteria in the soil are sluggish with the cold. This is sometimes thought a disadvantage, but it isn't really. It means you can dig in your manure at any convenient time, knowing that its goodness will be held in readiness until the weather warms up and your new tomato plants start looking for it. You can't do that with chemical fertilisers.

Manure Tea

If you feel that your tomato plants would benefit from a quick boost, then manure tea is a great way to encourage them. Simply put a couple of shovelfuls of manure into a Hessian bag and then steep it like an outsize teabag in a garbage bin full of water for a day or two until the water is the colour of weak tea. Don't use it on dry soil, however as it may be too concentrated.

Keep the lid on the garbage bin, the brew smells and will attract flies. It will keep for a week or so, or you can pour any leftovers on the compost heap, along with the contents of the used 'teabag.

Blood and Bone

Blood and bone isn't strictly manure, it is a by-product of

the meat industry. It is useful for a quick boost, being rich in nitrogen and phosphorus. It is nearly as concentrated as a chemical so it should be used by the cupful rather than the bucketful. Water it in at once in case it burns the plants, and most of the smell will go away.

The blood in blood and bone provides the nitrogen; bone meal on its own gives the phosphorus. It is the richest organic source of the element and releases its nitrogen and phosphorus very slowly so there is no danger of phosphates contaminating ground water or polluting creeks and rivers. You need to apply it only occasionally: a generous dressing should last at least a couple of years.

Controlling pests and diseases

Plant health starts with the soil. If the soil is healthy, with lots of humus and the micro-organisms that live in it, the plants that grow in it will be healthy and able to shake off pests with little assistance. Just how the micro-organisms help isn't perfectly understood: it is thought that they make antibiotic substances and vitamins that help in disease resistance. Healthy soils contain lots of beneficial microorganisms that kill pathogenic microbes.

Tomatoes are subject to a number of viruses, for which there is no known cure. It is thought that viruses are spread by aphids, so control of these vigorous breeders is important. A strong squirt from the hose will knock them senseless and they rarely crawl back again or you can squash them. If you miss them and a plague builds up, pyrethrum, tobacco water

Manure or compost tea gives your plants a healthy drink

or soft soap will dispatch them most efficiently.

Pyrethrum is a botanical insecticide which is derived from the flowers of an African species of chrysanthemum. It is the usual active ingredient in fly sprays. Be careful when spraying it near a pond as it is poisonous to fish.

A strong froth of soapy water kills insects, but be sure to use soft soap based on potassium rather than ordinary soap based on sodium, a substance you don't want to add to your soil. Adding a little soft soap to other insecticides helps them stick to the plant and the bugs.

Caterpillars love tomatoes and can be tricky to control. The fastest way is to squash them as soon as you see them. Derris is also effective. Derris is an extract of the roots of a tropical vine. It is a stomach poison – the caterpillar eats a bit of poisoned leaf and dies. It is usually dusted on as a dry powder rather than mixed with water and sprayed. It is however very poisonous to fish. One of the most effective methods of combating caterpillars is through germ warfare. You spray the caterpillars with the milky spore disease Bacillus thuringiensis which is deadly to caterpillars but not to birds or people.

Snails also love tomatoes and need to be controlled. Commercial snail baits are effective, but the snail takes a while to die and in the meantime might be eaten by a bird or lizard which may also be poisoned. It is safer to sprinkle the snails or slugs with salt. You can protect tender young tomato seedlings by surrounding them with a snail-proof barrier of ash,

sharp poultry grit or chopped up hair. You can also trap them by tipping some beer into juice bottles (laid on their side with an opening cut out) or into left over orange or grapefruit half skins. You have to keep topping up the beer, and drowned snails are not the prettiest sight, so toss them into the compost heap.

Other remedies – neem or margosa oil has long been used as an insecticide in India and proponents argue that it is very effective against just about every insect. Many organic gardeners also swear by garlic water, made by crushing three or four cloves garlic and infusing them in half a litre of hot water until cool and suitably smelly. It is most effective against soft-bodied insects such as aphids or bean fly.

Seed / seedling selection

Organic growers generally prefer non-hybrid tomatoes.

When buying seedlings choose young, strong seedlings which are not too tall and spindly. They should not have flowers or fruit on them, and ensure that the leaves are a dark green colour with no purple discoloration.

Crop rotation

It is important for all vegetable growing to rotate the type of vegetable that you grow on the patch. This will minimise the risk of diseases and nematodes.

As a rule of thumb, plant an above ground crop alternated with a below the ground crop. Tomatoes, capsicums, chillies, eggplant and potatoes all belong to the same family which is the nightshade (solanaceous) family,

Neem Oil is registered for use as an organic pesticide in many countries

and ideally should not be grown within three years of each other. However, if you are careful with crop hygiene and keeping your plant site healthy with compost and manure, you may be able to get away with a smaller rotation period.

Planting

Dipping your seedling plug into a solution of seaweed will boost root growth. Before planting, pinch off the bottom leaves and bury as much as possible of the lower stem. This will encourage more roots to grow up the stem which should give you larger, healthier plants. Once planted and firmed into the ground, give your seedlings a good watering and then mulch them.

Some gardeners recommend cutting a few leafy branches and putting those over the seedlings like tee pees to prevent scorch. Over a couple of days, the leaves slowly fall off so that the seedlings get gradually increasing exposure to the sun, thus minimising any transplant shock.

Companion Planting

Companion planting is planting two or more species that coexist to mutual benefit and do so with overlapping root zones. Anything planted as a companion to tomato should be a moderate feeder and have a relatively small leaf area. You would not plant pumpkin beside tomato because it is a heavy feeder and has a massive leaf surface area. The same logic applies to corn since it is a heavy feeder and requires full sunlight.

The idea that some plants exert a beneficial effect on others growing nearby and other plants exert a malign influence

is an ancient one that is now receiving renewed attention. French marigolds (Tagetes patula) secret an enzyme or a hormone into the soil that deters nematodes from infesting their roots and it seems that planting them next to tomatoes will help protect them.

Other good companions for tomatoes are basil, chives, parsley and onions which are good for pest control. Companion plants can be planted in rows between the tomatoes.

Foliar Feeding

Tomatoes love seaweed sprays – which are ideally sprayed about 10 – 14 days after planting. They can be applied once a month thereafter if desired. Tomatoes also enjoy comfrey tea sprayed onto them as well as other feeds such as fish emulsion or liquid worm casting extracts. Liquid manures can also be used, but take care not to make them too strong. Mix up 25% well broken down manure with 75% water.

Your tomatoes should be fed about once every 14 days, and once they have fruit they should be fed once a week, preferably late in the day so that they can absorb the nutrients at night.

If your plants are a bit pale in colour, give them a feed of liquid fertiliser.

Hygiene

Hygiene in the garden is very important for organic growers. Without care, pests and diseases will build up to levels that cannot be controlled.

Diseased plants and rotting fruits will attract pests and diseases. Ensure that all fallen leaves and fruits are carefully

Planting marigolds next to tomatoes helps deter nematodes

Basil, chives, parsley and onions planted near tomatoes provide pest control

collected and either sealed into a plastic bag and disposed of in the rubbish bin, or buried. DO NOT place them on top of the compost heap because the spores and young pests on them will move back onto your fine tomato crop.

When your tomato crop is finished, dig up as many of the roots as possible and dispose of them in the above manner.

Fruit fly

Some organic gardeners use a thin rag, like a handkerchief, to cover their fruit to prevent fruit fly causing a problem. Picking the fruits when they are just beginning to colour also lowers the risk of fruit fly attack. There are baits available to attract the fruit fly away from the tomatoes, however few of these are organic.

Tasty tomatoes

After nursing your tomatoes for 60 – 90 days, you should have the best tasting tomatoes ever.

The flavour of tomatoes is determined by sweet or sourness as well as aroma. Constituents of the fruit such as the sugars, sucrose and glucose are the main determinants of sweetness, whilst organic acids such as citrate determine the sourness. Over 400 volatile compounds have been found in tomatoes and these help to impart their flavour.

Defining the flavour of a tomato is a complex thing. Flavour is different for everyone and may be related to people's psychological perceptions. A particular flavour may be related to a bygone memory, a good or bad experience and how it is savoured by the tongue. The tongue tastes sweet, sour, salt and bitter. In conjunction with this and aroma detected by the nose, the brain collates the information and gives a perception of flavour.

Because you have grown your own tomatoes and given them plenty of good, organic nutrients and lots of care and all the things that you believe make tasty tomatoes, they should have a wonderful flavour.

Does the moon influence tomato growth?

Planting by the moon is a method that has been practised in rural communities for over two thousand years. It is believed that planting by the phases of the Moon provides a superior garden. Seeds germinate faster. Plants are hardier and more disease-resistant. They blossom sooner and bear more fruit.

Just as importantly, they better resist the stress of harsh weather, drought and insect infestation. We have not tried this yet, but we include this information because it is widely practised in rural communities and many people swear by it.

What are the moon's phases?

The moon waxes (increases) and wanes (decreases) over a period of about twenty-eight days.

This cycle from New Moon to New Moon is called the lunation cycle and is divided into four parts commonly called quarters or phases.

The best way to use moon gardening techniques is to buy a special calendar. Fortunately, so many modern gardeners use

Organically grown tomatoes are free of chemicals

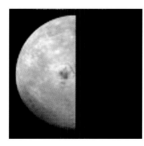

moon planting, that calendars are generally available in good gardening shops in most areas. You can also buy then on-line. Other sources for Moon phase information are the weather page of your local newspaper, almanacs and gardening magazines.

FIRST QUARTER: The first quarter/phase begins at New Moon. Many calendars will show it as a blackened moon (dead moon) indicating that there is no moonlight to be seen on the first night since the moon lies between the earth and the sun. The New Moon is waxing and is a time for new beginnings that favour personal growth and in the garden it is time for germination. The Earth begins to breathe in.

SECOND QUARTER: The second quarter/phase starts about seven-plus days after the New Moon and ends with the Full Moon. The sun and moon are ninety degrees apart. The waxing powers of the moon are especially strong at this time - more births come into this world during this phase. This is the best quarter for planting tomatoes.

THIRD QUARTER: The third quarter/phase begins at Full Moon - the moon has covered half of its journey around the Earth. This is when the sun and moon are opposite and sunlight shines fully on the moon. Calendars often indicate this day as white full moon. The Full Moon stands for illumination, completion and unrest. Fertilize (organic) during the 3rd or 4th quarter when the moon is in a water sign.

FOURTH QUARTER: The fourth quarter/phase begins halfway (about twenty-one days into the lunation cycle) between the Full Moon and next New Moon. The sun and moon are again at ninety degrees apart and the waning powers of the moon are especially weak. This phase is a time of reorganization, reflection and riddling oneself of unnecessary things in order to make room for the coming New Moon. Cultivate the soil, weed the garden, employ pest management and remove unwanted plants.

Anyone who sees the tides change due to the pull of the Moon's gravity on earth will not doubt the influence of the Moon on daily life. Similarly you can observe the same rhythms in the rising and falling of sap in plants, in changes in weather and rainfall. If you are interested in learning more about gardening by the moon we suggest that you consult one of the many web sites or books available on this subject.

Transplanting tomatoes is best done during the second quarter

14. Hydroponics

Hydroponics is the practice of growing plants in a medium, other than soil, using a nutrient solution of materials essential to plants dissolved in water.

No food plant responds more satisfactorily to hydroponic culture (inside, under high-powered lights, fed specially concocted nutrient solutions) than tomatoes.

Hydroponic gardening is an easy, environmentally-friendly way to grow a wide variety of healthy plants in a relatively small space. The benefits of growing hydroponically include:

- Hydroponic plants grow more rapidly than plants in soil because it has direct access to essential plant nutrients and water and other plants don't have to compete for nutrients as plants in soil do.

- Hydroponic indoor gardening is possible year-round.

- Hydroponics are efficient as the plants do not have to go searching for food ... it is supplied virtually as a "smorgasbord" (the plants take up what they need).

- Hydroponic plants are grown in a relatively disease-free, pest-free medium.

- Hydroponic plants can be grown in small spaces - in closets, on apartment balconies, on kitchen counters and in classrooms.

- Hydroponic plant roots are fixed to the growing media, or grow trays, giving them unlimited access to nutrients. This results in plants that yield superior vegetables and flowers with smaller roots, compared to plants grown in soil.

- Hydroponics make gardening possible in low soiled areas, rocky terrains and small spaces like apartment balconies.

- Hydroponics makes gardening possible indoors with artificial lighting.

- Hydroponics demands less labour - no digging, soil maintenance or weeding is required.

You can purchase hydroponic equipment from hydroponic shops, or you can set up your own. Some of the more popular tomato varieties grown hydroponically include Apollo, Belmondo, Caruso, Dombito, Larma, Perfecto, Trend and Trust

However setting up and getting the watering and nutrient system working correctly is quite an involved subject and outside the scope of this book. We suggest you visit your local hydroponic centre if you would like to learn more.

15. Common Tomato Terms

Beefsteak	The primo slicer for sandwiches, cooking Beefsteaks are the very biggest tomatoes. Their pulp cavity is usually small, and always compressed and distorted by the extensive placenta wall, giving the 'marbled' appearance of a steak. Because of the compressed pulp cavity and networking of the fruit wall as placenta, beefsteaks hold together well when sliced, and together with their large size, make them the ideal 'slicer' for sandwiches. Their high fruit wall to pulp ratio means they also cook down well for sauces. There is a lot of variation between varieties in the density of the flesh, juiciness (i.e. firm or very soft when ripe), and in the size and softness of the central 'core'. Flavour can vary according to the ratio of sugars to acids, and according to the relative amount of sugar or acid present.
Cherry	These tomatoes vary from pea sized up to where they tip over into the small 'salad' type. They are usually very prolific, and some have been bred for high sugars as a snacking 'fruit'. They are very colourful as a whole tomato in a salad and their size makes them ideally suited to this purpose.
Chlorosis	The yellowing or whitening of normally green plant tissue because of a decreased amount of chlorophyll, often as a result of disease or nutrient deficiency
Determinate	This means the fruit all ripens at the same time making them ideal for commercial harvesting. Determinate plants are seldom staked as the plant tends to have a bush shaped growth. Tomato cages are one solution that many gardeners use to get the plant off the ground without having to stake.
Fast ripening	Any tomato that starts producing it's crop of ripe fruit within about 3-4 months of first sowing the seed.
Heirloom	Old variety which has been maintained either because it has appealing attributes like extra large size, unusual colouring, special connoisseur qualities, or because of family sentimental reasons.

Hybrid	This is a variety created by deliberately and painstakingly taking pollen from an existing open pollinated tomato and putting it onto a different open pollinated tomato. The seed gives a first generation (F1) that is extremely uniform. But keeping seed and resowing it gives a highly varied and non-uniform lot The advantage of hybrids is vigour and the ability to use a parent known to be disease resistant.
Indeterminate	This is the opposite of determinate. These plants continue to grow and continue to produce new flowers for as long as they are alive. They will ripen their fruit over the entire length of the growing season. Ripening starts with the bottom trusses (the term for a cluster of tomatoes) and continues up the vine. Indeterminate plants are excellent candidates for staking as their vine-like growth constantly produces fruit over the entire growing season
Late variety	A tomato that doesn't start ripening fruit for more than 5 months from seed sowing
Main season	A tomato that starts producing ripe fruit from about 4 months of first sowing the seed.
Open pollinated	Usually (but not always) older varieties where no artificial crossing or pollination has taken place.
Paste or Plum	Paste tomatoes often have fine thick flesh and reduced amounts of pulp. This makes them good for holding shape when canned, and it means they also slice quite well. Paste tomatoes are characterized by possessing high amounts of sugars and acids (flavour), a lot of pectin, and less water than other tomato types. The higher amount of pectin, coupled with the lower amount of water makes the juice thicker requiring less time to cook down to a paste consistency. Additionally, growing conditions have a direct influence on the final product. Feeding and watering is reduced as the crop nears maturity.
Petiole	The slender stem that supports the blade of a leaf.

References

A number of references were used to compile this book including:

AVRDC: www.avrdc.org

Blazey, C, The Australian Vegetable Garden, 1999, Australia

Clemson University: www.clemson.edu

Colorado State University: www.colostate.edu

Cornell University: www.cornell.edu

Dept of Primary Industries & Fisheries. Qld: www2.dpi.qld.gov.au/business/8725.html

Diggers Club: www.diggers.com.au

eSeeds: www.eseeds.com

Epstein, E. and Bloom, A.J. (2005) Mineral Nutrition of Plants: Principles and Perspectives. Second Edition, Sinauer Associates, Sunderland

Gardening with Greenfingers Malcolm Campbell: www.greenfingers.com.au

Heirloom Tomato Plants: www.heirloomtomatoplants.com

High Mowing Organic Seeds: www.highmowingseeds.com

Landreth Seeds: www.landrethseeds.com

Mother Earth News: www.motherearthnews.com

www.naturalhub.com/grow_vegetable_cultivars_tomato.htm

North Carolina State University: www.ncsu.edu

Ohio State University: www.osu.edu

Office of International Research, Education and Development, Virginia Tech: www.oired.vt.edu

Ontario Ministry of Agriculture, Food and Rural Affairs: www.omafra.gov.on.ca

Oregon State University: www.oregonstate.edu

Park Seed: www.parkseed.com

Practical Guide to Organic Gardening, Better Homes and Gardens, 1998, Australia

Purdue University: www.purdue.edu

Rachel's Supplies: www.rachelssupply.com

Seed Savers Exchange: www.seedsavers.org

Seeds Trust: www.seedstrust.com

Selected Plants: www.selectedplants.com

Sweet Tomato Test Garden: www.sweettomatotestgarden.com

The Tasteful Garden: www.tastefulgarden.com

Texas A & M University: www.tamu.edu

Tomato: www.tomato.com.au

Totally Tomatoes: www.totallytomato.com

University of California CE - Santa Clara County: www.mastergardeners.org

University of California Davis: www.ucdavis.edu

University of Florida: www.ufl.edu

University of Guelph: www.uoguelph.ca

University of Kansas: www.ku.edu

University of Massachusetts: www.umass.edu

US Dept Agriculture: Agricultural Research Service: www.ars.usda.gov

Yates Pty Ltd, Yates Garden Guide, 2000, Sydney

Your notes